"Saddleback Church is built on a strong foundation of men—strong, respected, godly men who lead by authentic example, through honest communication and inspirational action in our church. In *Sleeping Giant*, my men's pastor Kenny Luck gives you a local church blueprint for moving men from being an audience sitting in a seat to becoming an army marching on the field in your congregation. Discover the pathway to engaging the men in your church to be all God intended them to be as they serve as leaders, counselors, shepherds, husbands, and fathers. *Sleeping Giant* shares the secret to building a healthy leader-making growth and development engine that supports the vision of your church."

—Rick Warren, founding pastor, Saddleback Church and author of *The Purpose Driven Life*

"*Sleeping Giant* does what it infers—awakening men to their calling and potential. Every pastor, church, and leader that desires to activate men for God's work should read this book, and so should every man. It's a life-changer and a church-changer."

—George O. Wood, general superintendent, The General Council of the Assemblies of God

"Kenny takes on the monumental task of rightly charging men with their biblical roles as husbands, leaders, fathers, and much more. He examines the current trends of media and society that continually push men into a less than masculine role and contrasts them with God's design for men. Kenny has written a great book that can lead men and men's ministries to the rightful place in God's economy."

—Bryant Wright, president of the Southern Baptist Convention and senior pastor, Johnson Ferry Baptist Church, Marietta, Georgia

"We were struggling to establish a dynamic men's ministry. That is no longer the case. Our church now has new men's small groups meeting weekly, with plans for expansion and leadership development in the future thanks to Kenny's model represented in *Sleeping Giant*. It started a revolution that infected our men, their marriages, and our overall leadership."

—Kevin Springer pastor of life development, Living Oaks Community Church, Newbury Park, California, and author of *Power Evangelism*

"The mission of God advances most powerfully when God's men are engaged and deployed. As the church has struggled to enlist men over the past decades, Kenny Luck has faithfully and effectively led an army of men in the mission of God. *Sleeping Giant* skillfully shows church leaders how to reach and launch men into a world of great need for God's great glory. Devour this book!"

—Thom S. Rainer, president and CEO,
LifeWay Christian Resources

"*Sleeping Giant* is a masterpiece! As I read it my heart leaped inside. I can't wait for pastors and men's ministry leaders to begin using it to awaken the sleeping giant in their churches and communities to reach and transform broken culture."

—Keith Burkhart, Baptist General Convention,
Family and Men's Ministry

"I loved it! I have been working with men for the past twenty years of my life and this book is the best book on how to minister to I have read, because it comes from someone who is actually doing it in the context of the local church. It is a must read for any pastor or leader serious about awakening the sleeping giant of the church—the men. Thank you, Kenny."

—Steve Sonderman, associate pastor of men's ministry, Elmbrook Church, Brookfield, Wisconsin, and founder of No Regrets Men's Ministry

"In *Sleeping Giant* Kenny puts his finger on the pulse of where masculinity is today, correctly diagnosing the challenges before the church, and giving the church a solid course of action to activate men for their kingdom mission. *Sleeping Giant* will move men from the audiences of the church to the armies of the church, unleashing the '800-pound Gorilla' for battle. I believe this could lead to a worldwide revival of men and the church!"

—Kevin Trick, community pastor-men's ministry,
Centre Street Church, Calgary, Alberta

"Kenny Luck has a proven track record of raising up a generation of godly men and equipping them to make a difference. *Sleeping Giant* is solid, empowering, and biblical. I highly recommend this book for you and your church."

—Chris Hodges, founding and senior pastor, Church of the Highlands

"This book is neither flamboyant nor extravagant . . . it's not melodramatic or controversial—it is simply *helpful*. Few books that I have seen in recent years so explores unexplored potential in the church as this one does. Kenny Luck has offered an opportunity that we must not miss. Here is *help* for all of us, don't miss it!"

—Rev. Dr. Clive Calver, senior pastor, Walnut Hill Community Church, Bethel, Connecticut, and former president of World Relief

"Church ministry can be all consuming. The opportunities and the needs seem endless. Rarely does the servant leader have the legitimate chance to step aside and reflect on the dreams that brought him into ministry. I am here to tell you that *Sleeping Giant* will fuel new dreams for your ministry. What would it look like if the men in and around your church began to operate fully under the lordship of Christ, become spiritual leaders in their homes, and then out of their homes, stand tall for Christ in the community and enthusiastically align the vision and mission for your church? Wow! I would urge you to allow God to use Kenny Luck and *Sleeping Giant* to fuel these dreams."

—Brian Doyle, founder and president of Iron Sharpens Iron

"Many books contain filler you have to dig through to find the nuggets of truth. No so in *Sleeping Giant*. I found it impossible to run or skip through the book; instead I had to walk slowly, stop and think, and even sit a while and reflect on the insights that touched my mind and my heart. *Sleeping Giant* opens the wound many churches are ignoring or covering over and provides strong medicine for not only healing but for thriving. I appreciate how Kenny speaks from a wealth of practical, hands on experiences with real men in real churches. No theoretical solutions, unrealistic suggestions or guilt tripping here. Thank you Kenny for caring enough about the church and God's people to help put our feet back on the right track."

—Tom Blackaby, coauthor of *The Man God Uses*, *The Family God Uses*, and many others and international director of Blackaby Ministries International

"Unless the American church seriously overhauls its approach to reaching and teaching men, our country may be in for a long spiritual winter. *Sleeping Giant* is a great resource to help us identify and solve one of our nation's most urgent needs—calling and equipping men to lead God-centered lives."

—Mark Merrill, president, Family First and All Pro Dad

"Kenny Luck makes the statement in *Sleeping Giant*, 'Inspiration without progression leads to confusion.' This is true in so many churches with men's groups. We inspire men but then don't give an outlet for action. *Sleeping Giant* is the action step. Our church just recently started applying the action steps of Get In, Get Healthy, Get Strong, and Get Going in our weekly men's small groups. It has been a transformational moment in the history of our men's group. I highly recommend *Sleeping Giant*. It will transform the men in your church, their homes, and their community.

—Rick Friesen, executive pastor,
Abundant Life Baptist Church, Lee's Summit, Missouri

"As one of the most respected men's ministry leaders in the country, Luck has taken his years of hard-earned experience to create a rare and effective resource for pastors who struggle to enlist men into God's magnanimous will. I especially appreciate his emphasis on justice in *Sleeping Giant*, which is so important to God and to male spirituality. Consume this manifesto. Deploy its power today."

—Paul Coughlin, author of *No More Christian Nice Guy* and founder of
The Protectors: Freedom From Bullying—Courage and Character for Life

"Life is a game and we are the players. Having a *Game Plan for Life* continues to be my message for men. In *Sleeping Giant*, Kenny gives us a view of the team that was 2-14 and missed the playoffs. When the players caught the vision of the coach and worked together for the same goal, they found themselves competing for a championship. The time is now for men in the church to get up and get in the game!"

—Joe Gibbs, three-time Super Bowl winning NFL coach,
three-time NASCAR Championship team owner, and two-time
NHRA Pro Stock team owner, and author of *Game Plan for Life*

"I think it's obvious in today's family unit that most men have fumbled the ball in their role as spiritual leader. Kenny Luck shares with us the right game plan for men to re-establish their God ordained responsibilities. I highly recommend this book for any pastor, husband, father, or young man who wants to be a godly role model in today's society."

—Tommy Bowden, FOX sports analyst and
former head football coach, Clemson University

"Too often, in today's politically correct culture, men have become afraid to step out into spiritual leadership. Kenny Luck's *Sleeping Giant* is a wake-up call. It's a manifesto for the kind of difference men can make when they're unafraid to make a difference."

—Phil Cooke, filmmaker, media consultant, and
author of *Jolt! Get the Jump on a World That's Constantly Changing*

"*Sleeping Giant* calls out to awaken men in the church today. As Jethro challenged Moses, 'What you are doing is not good' (Exod. 18:17), even Moses needed leaders around him; and those leaders were waiting and ready to be called. We need to see men activated and raised up together to carry the mantle of leadership in our areas of influence. It's going to take men stirred from their slumber—encouraged, equipped, empowered, then released as men of strength and full of courage. *Sleeping Giant* will awaken and ignite the men of the church."

—Russell Verhey, men's pastor,
New Life Church, Colorado Springs, Colorado

"Since the moment God created Adam and gave him 'dominion' over the earth, God has put 'conquering energy' inside the heart of every man. While this 'conquering energy' has at times through history been used for evil—God intended it to be used for good. There is an 'unstoppable' force for good that is lying dormant in our society! That unstoppable God given force is lying dormant inside our churches. In a society that has marginalized the role of men that 'unstoppable' force for good is lying dormant inside of men. But *Sleeping Giant* promises to be an "awakening"! Men are waking up all over America to their true identity and are embarking on a journey to their God-given destiny! Men were born for battle. With Kenny Luck's help they will learn to fight the right ones! The battle for our family, for God's glory, and for eternity! Let America's warriors wake up!"

—Phil Hopper, senior pastor,
Abundant Life Baptist Church, Lee's Summit, Missouri

"There is no greater need in the church today than to mobilize God's men for kingdom work. With *Sleeping Giant*, Kenny Luck has provided the body of Christ with a catalyst for unleashing the explosive power of truly discipled men—and not a moment too soon."

—Chris Shirley, Ph.D., assistant professor of Adult Ministry,
Southwestern Baptist Theological Seminary, Fort Worth, Texas

Pastor Jim,

I'm tired of being a bleacher guy w/tendancies of being a thermo nuclear man, leaving death & destruction in my wake. I encourage you to read & take heed or we men of UBF will all become bleacher men & Thermo nuclear men left to our own worldly devices.

Respectfully,

Richard Ambre

Sleeping
GIANT

Sleeping GIANT

No Movement of God without Men of God

Kenny Luck

with Tom Crick

B&H
PUBLISHING GROUP

NASHVILLE, TENNESSEE

Contents

A Word for Pastors and for Their Men

To all of our fellow local church pastors,

This book is dedicated to serving you! We have spent the last ten years serving our pastor, Rick Warren (perhaps trying to keep up with him is a better way to put it), by raising up leaders and forming the ranks of our men around the vision God has planted in our pastor. This is the essence of what Sleeping Giant is all about—serving the local pastor by helping to activate his men around the vision God has called him to fulfill. We hope to do that in the pages that follow by helping you see the powerful cultural, biblical, and spiritual relevance of meaningful ministry to men in your part of the world and then equipping you with the simple strategies and tools for you to apply *in your church context*.

We have trained thousands of pastors from all over the world and from various denominations and church structures who are applying with great success what you will be learning. The key for these churches is that they prayerfully listened to God while considering or reconsidering men and their role in a local body of believers. As you begin to engage this material God will begin to put faces in your mind of laymen He is calling to help you build your leadership team as well as give you new thoughts as to how to invest your men in the vision of your church. Write those names down! God is raising up the men you need (some are still unbelievers at this moment) for you to be successful in your mission. Make sure you have a notepad ready or just write in the margins of this book because God *is* going to speak to you. He is going to speak names of men into your mind. He is going to speak to you through faces and images of men. He is going to speak to you from your own journey as a man. He is going to speak to you through the women in your church and community who desperately need healthier men. Most important, God is going to speak to you directly through the Holy Spirit and through His Word that you love so deeply.

Be ready.

If you are a layman in a church, a volunteer in men's ministry, or a men's ministry leader in your church, your job is simple: engage the material, the exercises, and the strategy for the purpose of producing healthy men and healthy leaders for your pastor. More than anything that's what he needs to fulfill the vision God has called him to accomplish. He cannot do it alone and he needs you!

We are here to help you awaken the Sleeping Giant in your congregation and community.

The world is waiting,

Kenny Luck and Tom Crick

Chapter 1

The "Resonating Revival"

"The good man brings good things out of the good stored up in him, and the evil man brings evil things out of the evil stored up in him."

MATTHEW 12:35

Everybody gets it.

When a man's character and conduct become healthy, *it changes things*. Most directly, the women and children connected to their life and choices suffer less and develop better. Fewer literal and emotional orphans fall prey to evil cultural predators who exploit their loneliness, needs, and insecurities for evil purposes. Negative generational and cultural cycles of chaos, dysfunction, and destruction are interrupted. In the crudest analysis, when native sons have the capacity to act in the interests of others versus solely acting in the interest of themselves, the foundational infrastructures of societies and nations change. Wherever these

> When native sons have the capacity to act in the interests of others, the foundational infrastructures of societies and nations change.

men go, their character goes with them. Professional, political, social, cultural, and religious infrastructures become the beneficiaries of well-formed men; and, as a consequence, those same organizations become less corrupt and produce fewer cynics. Maybe your family, your country, your community, or your church could use a few more men like this. Men who bring hope by their very presence.

Intuitively, everyone knows that healthy and moral men are like sticks of dynamite: they can create blast zones of life that extend far into the fabric of the society in which they find themselves. Equally true is that those same sticks of dynamite can go off and produce blast zones of death and massive collateral suffering as men self-preserve, self-protect, self-indulge, and seek to be self-important at the expense of others. This powerful and dangerous potential has always been disappointing to a loving Father who watches His sons expectantly, hoping for a healthy expression of His character in the lives of others. Scripture tells us that the blast zones of male character and conduct both break God's heart and boil His blood. *"The vineyard of the Lord Almighty is the nation of Israel, and the men of Judah are the garden of his delight. And he looked for justice, but saw bloodshed; for righteousness, but heard cries of distress"* (Isa. 5:7).

Among the current social commentaries and studies reported, you might have seen or heard these recent features in major periodicals and Web platforms:

- *The Wall Street Journal* asked: "Where Have All the Good Men Gone?"[1]
- *Newsweek* shouted: "Man Up! Re-thinking Masculinity."[2]
- *The Atlantic* announced: "The End of Men."[3]
- *The New York Times* observed: "Downsized and Downtrodden, Men Are the New Women."[4]
- *Fast Company* felt compelled to make "The Case for Girls."[5]
- "The Demise of Guys" was presented by Dr. Philip Zombardo at the world renowned TED Conference.[6]
- In a moment of clarity, *Time* magazine called out the Hollywood caricature of perennially adolescent men in "Land of the Lost: Delusions of Manhood."[7]

- CNN answered the present and pervading cultural sense of loss with the headline: *"Why Men Are in Trouble"*[8]

For every one of these major news stories, thousands of others were flooding Web channels, blogs, Web sites, local newspapers, and TV outlets that detailed both the spiraling and negative outcomes flowing out of the beliefs and behaviors of men around the world. Pick up the paper or click onto a major news outlet, and within seconds one can lament the men, whether it is sexual violence against women in Uganda and human trafficking in Thailand or Wall Street greed and epidemic fatherlessness in the United States. The information age has virtually crushed the ability of men, male culture, and masculinity worldwide to escape the one thing it has relied on for centuries: *staying invisible*. Men do not like to be exposed or made to feel guilty; and yet now a very simple but powerful global realization has occurred: suffering makes the news, and the behaviors of men are at the center of most of the suffering.

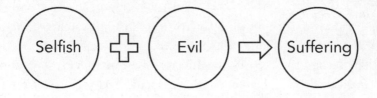

This is the first factor every church needs to be aware of when it comes to the resonating revival that is coming through men. Pain resonates deeply, and any person, group of people, or organization that successfully reduces suffering through touching and transforming men in their community becomes immediately relevant. As the church attempts to reach people, it should be asking: "What *pervasive, unresolved* problems can we solve that dramatically impact the people and communities we are trying to reach?"

Answer: mobilize the *unactivated* men of your church and the yet *unsaved* men in your community. (We will show you how to do this in Section III.)

Reactions vs. Solutions

In the politically charged arena of global activism, pointing out the Sleeping Giant publicly can be risky. Waiting my turn to speak at a justice conference, I listened to a nation-ally known expert in human trafficking who told a moving story of her exposure to the child sex trade in Cambodia. The screen behind her flashed scenes from the very streets she walked, which shook her soul and launched her into a deeper involvement with the justice movement. Her research was the second act. Profound and disturbing statistics about human traf-ficking locally, nationally, and globally had the audience by the throat. Her last plea to the audience was to not sit idly by but to get involved. I listened closely as she outlined simple ways people could get involved from raising awareness to rescu-ing victims to rehabilitating those rescued.

> Any person, group of people, or organization that successfully reduces suffering through touching and transforming men becomes relevant.

The second speaker was the director of an international organiza-tion dedicated to helping churches understand and implement orphan care ministries. Like the first woman she, too, was over the top and excellent. Articulate, passionate, and research oriented. The audience was captivated and so was I, especially when she said, "The orphan epidemic is a symptom of the HIV epidemic in Africa where whole generations of parents are being wiped out and the children are made vulnerable and left to take care of themselves."

It was my turn now.

I started by saying how much I loved and admired the first two speakers but then said, "But I have to respectfully disagree with their solutions." You could hear a pin drop. I carefully went on to explain that we can raise awareness of these issues, we can rescue and restore people, as well as rehabilitate and reintegrate the victims into society. "All of these," I went on to say, "need to be done, but these are reactions *not* solutions." At this point my neck was stretched so far out in that room you could have cut off my head with a pair of scissors. So I took a big, deep breath and let it out: "The eight-hunderd-pound gorilla in the room when it comes to the church worldwide and its ability to deliver social justice will be directly related to its ability to effectively evangelize, equip, disciple, and deploy men to reach other men. You can skim the surface of an oil spill all day long, feel good about your work, and point to all the oil you have scooped up. But until you cap that well below the surface, it is fantasy to think you have made real prog-

> We need a church-to-church movement that helps men get into a relationship with God.

ress toward a solution." I wasn't done with my little rant. "Ninety-nine percent of the energy, investment, and activism is spent on the reaction side to broken male culture with no attempts on anyone's part to actually go after the man himself. That is why we need a church-to-church movement that helps men get into a relationship with God, get healthy as a man, get strong as a believer, and get going into his community. Do that and you *take away demand, deal with the source, and deliver hope that goes beyond relief to sustainable generational impact.* When God's people do that in combination with the other efforts, then we can begin to use the word *solution.* Helping victims of broken male culture is not the *solution.* Changed men with changed identities and a higher allegiance who are able to rise above the cultures that have trained them to make others suffer will be the time we can truly celebrate." Then something shocking happened: spontaneous and continuous applause.

Everyone MOST *definitely* gets it.

Black Velvet and Dazzling Diamonds

I was dazzled.

I was only twenty-four years old when my dad loaned me money so that I could have enough to buy a stone that, to this day, rests proudly on my wife's left ring finger. I had never done anything like this before, and

I was afraid of getting ripped off. This was big. As the jeweler popped the hood of his briefcase, I was expecting to see a small bag holding the diamonds, but instead he produced a thick, black-velvet place mat. After moving the briefcase over to the side, the jeweler slid the place mat directly in front of me and asked, "Are you ready to find the diamond that is going to go on your bride's finger?" No words. My smile back said it all. Then, like stars lighting up a jet black night, he slowly moved the bag from left to right across the black velvet, depositing tens of thousands of dollars worth of diamonds in front of me. What a showman and, I confess, what an effect. Against that black velvet I could see every cut and every facet of every diamond without struggling. Without that pad every diamond would have lost it's glory, but with it each stone put forth it's own unique sparkle. The blackness was necessary for the brilliance.

As I have traveled the world, I have found God to be somewhat like my jeweler friend when it comes to how He chooses to bring His glory and salvation among men in particular. The black backdrop of men cooperating with evil provides the contrast for a shining movement of men who stand out and manifest the glory of God through their trans- formation.

First, and most painfully, the black backdrop.

- One out of every three women worldwide will be raped, beaten, coerced into sex or otherwise abused in her lifetime.[9]
- 11.5 million single mothers in the U.S. are raising 20.1 million children by themselves.[10]
- 153 million orphans currently worldwide.[11]
- 33.3 million global HIV cases.[12]
- 26 million prostitutes.[13]
- Total market value of sexual trafficking estimated to be in excess of $32 billion annually.[14]
- There are more slaves today than were seized from Africa in four centuries of the trans-Atlantic slave trade.[15]
- 300 million children are subjected to hazardous physical labor, commercial sex, exploitation, and child trafficking.[16]
- $9.5 is the annual global revenue of the sale from trafficking human beings.[17]

- Human trafficking is second largest illegal criminal activity (second to drugs), but the fastest growing.[18]

These statistics do not begin to touch the secondary cesspools of injustice connected to the pornography, massage parlor, or sexual tourism industries. They also do not consider the largest and most widely accepted injustice connected to broken male culture—fatherlessness. In metro urban America teen drug use, incarceration, unwed teen pregnancy, and high school drop-out rates all quadruple in the face of a 70 percent rate of fatherless homes, according to the National Center for Fathering. From Bangkok to Wall Street, broken male culture is the wallpaper of modern journalism and human-interest stories. These metrics and movements as well as the monies that must be invested to support them have one thing in common: they are all painful outcomes related to male behavior currently covering the world.

The blast zone of these stories relates to millions of dissatisfied and disaffected women worldwide, who have been hurt or made to feel like second-class citizens. They are making news as well, actively seeking and achieving independence from men in these areas:

- emotional
- professional
- relational
- political
- financial
- spiritual

For the first time in world history, women outnumber men in both undergraduate and graduate degrees, in managerial positions, and in qualifying for the high-growth job sectors for the foreseeable future. Aggressive feminism asserts that men have actually become the new "ball and chain." Hollywood is banking on omega male for big box-office results, a new brand of man that is funny, hopelessly adolescent, and unable to be responsible.

> Hollywood is banking on omega male for big box-office results.

It's a heyday for misogynists.

All the negative exposure and isolating trends have added dark emotions to dark circumstances for men. Completely lacking moral authority, feeling no longer needed or able to provide, and not being turned to for emotional support, men around the world are running more than scared. In response, they are either withdrawing completely, filling with anger, or reacting with passivity—all of which cause more suffering.

Can it get any worse?

God's Diamonds in the Bag?

According to statistical experts, there are 2.1 billion Christians in the world. This means that there are between 500,000,000 and 700,000,000 affiliated Christian men roaming planet Earth.

Just as political uprisings have been dominating the news cycle across the Middle East, a similar dynamic is invading men's cultures across the globe, making a powerful case that not only is all not lost but that there is a huge upside to healthy, faith-led male counterculture. I see it in the Glovimo movement (which stands for Glory in Virginity Movement) in Uganda that has statistically lowered the HIV infection rate. I see it in the Joshua Generation movement in Brazil where young Christian men by the thousands are sending a new message to their culture by committing to a Christ-centered life of marital fidelity. I see it in the Sons of Congo movement where more than six thousand young men and boys are forming groups to be mentored spiritually and socially in Christ. I see it in the more than eight thousand men in small groups at my own church. I see men being called by the Holy Spirit into the justice movement. I see thousands of churches across the globe being called to invest in conferences and programs for its men. I see pastors turning to and telling their men how needed

> I see waves of good men making good decisions out of strong convictions about right and wrong in the little spaces of everyday life.

they are for the mission. I see men in small groups and life groups subgrouping to study the Word as men, talking honestly and accelerating their growth. I see waves of good men making good decisions out of strong convictions about right and wrong in the little spaces of everyday life. I see men of the church humbly forming ranks

> The hope of the world is the local church.

around their pastors and making themselves available for leader development and deployment. I see women and children in awe over the changes in their husbands and dads. I see men winning over temptation. I see men disciplining themselves toward relationships. I see men leading their families by example. I see men honoring women. I see men aggressively entering dark injustices and confronting evil in the open. What do we call a healthy men's culture where consistency of convictions is prevalent in numbers among men, bringing justice—and with justice, bringing hope?

You call that a *solution*.

The hope of the world is the local church, and the hope of the local church in this moment of history is the power of Christ residing in its men.

The Church with a Heart but No Spine

It's not that our sisters in Christ are inadequate to the fulfillment of the church's mission in this hour. Not at all. In fact, their patience and perseverance spiritually with us is going to be richly rewarded. Instead, it's that men who name the name of Jesus and have a heart for Him must also grow a spine for Him. There is nothing more pathetic than a Christian man who has a heart for God but no spine. How can it be that there are hundreds of millions of "Christian men," and yet the world cannot distinguish

> There is nothing more pathetic than a Christian man who has a heart for God but no spine.

them from the larger culture? Jesus Christ entered a broken male culture not unlike the ones that foster so much pain today and promptly started breaking the rules. While the first-century Jewish man thanked God that he wasn't a woman, a child, or a Gentile, Jesus made a point to connect with and bring dignity to all three. He had a spine. He spoke with the Samaritan woman. He had a spine. He told the disciples to let the children come. He had a spine. He defended the woman caught in adultery and stood between her and stones. He had a spine. He touched the physically unacceptable. He had a spine. He touched the ethnically unacceptable. He had a spine. He associated with the morally unacceptable. He had a spine.

> For the Son of Man, sympathy was *not* a substitute for action.

For the Son of Man, sympathy was *not* a substitute for action.

Similarly, nothing is more tragic than a church with a heart to do the work of Jesus but no muscle to pull it off. So many churches we have talked to register the same complaint: "We make the call and the men don't show up!" They declare it as if it is a man problem and not a church problem. The church is like the figurative man described in the first chapter of the book of James who fails to see reality when he looks in the mirror and walks away deluded about his condition. In the masculine context *deluded* is defined as making no deposits in men and then trying to write checks out of that account to advance church initiatives. Churches that are confused over the commitment of its men should take a hard look the church's own commitment to them as a marker. As pastors we can't expect strong energy and expression of our men to come from a weak connection and investment in them. The bottom line with your men is this: We will be showing you in the chapters to come how to change that. Pancake breakfasts and Father's Day mentions don't produce a lot of loyalty.

Can you blame them?

I was helping a confused church that had a robust weekend attendance come to grips with the low commitment of its men to a certain outreach and fading attendance at their men's meeting. After asking a few questions, I realized the highest vision this church had for its men was limited to attendance at a weekly morning study on campus that had run out of gas. There was no connection of the men's ministry to the larger mission and needs of the church for leaders, no process to take a man there, and no room in the men's circle for the guys who didn't fit the "committed" profile necessary to attend that study. Of course they had a weak response when they announced their outreach needs over the weekend at church. There was no clear vision, no pockets of deep relationships to pull on, and no intentional leader development.

> Relational capital is required in order to fund worthy initiatives with the energy and expressions of your men.

This discussion and many like them reflect another huge gorilla in the room of the church: *worthy initiatives are not enough.* Relational capital is required in order to fund worthy initiatives with the energy and expressions of your men. And relational capital does not materialize overnight. This church had a heart for initiatives and ministries the men could do but not a spine to actually invest in a meaningful vision, clear process, solid tools, and dedicated staff and volunteer structure that loved on the men. Meaningful relationships with your men and among your men are the Ebola virus of a strong men's community and wake the Sleeping Giant *already present in your church.* And that's the crux of the problem.

You can have men and not "*have*" them.

So whether you are a man reading this book who is ready to move from affiliated to activated or you are a pastor or men's leader who is ready to move your men from the audience to the army through meaningful relationships and a strong process, prepare to be both encouraged and challenged. This book is written to support the local church pastor as the local church pastor supports and invests in his men.

> The Activated Man: Dangerous but Good

Now it's time to spark the resonating revival.

Key Learnings

- Healthy men change the moral infrastructures of communities and countries at every level.
- Behaviors of men fuel cultural suffering.
- Transformed men reduce suffering and provide an opportunity for the church to be culturally relevant.
- Healthy men's communities in churches are igniting health worldwide.
- Healthy men evangelize, equip, and deploy men to reach other men.
- Churches need help to get men IN, HEALTHY, STRONG, and GOING back into their communities to deliver justice.
- The church can stem the tide of male withdrawal by becoming centers of masculine transformation.
- The church must provide its men with a strong vision, deep relationship, and intentional leadership development to be successful.

Chapter 2

The Eight-Hundred-
Pound Gorilla

*What you are doing is not good. You and these people
who come to you will only wear yourselves out. The work
is too heavy for you; you cannot handle it alone.*

EXODUS 18:17

Someone has to say *something*.

But many times no one says *anything*. This is why Hans Christian
Andersen's fable *The Emperor's New Clothes* has been translated into over
eighty languages.[19] It is the original parable that gave rise in modern
times to the "Pink Elephant" or "Eight-Hundred-Pound Gorilla" in the
room analogy. That is when every person present recognizes and sees
something wrong, but no one wants to point it out. Andersen's story
is the simple tale of two salesmen who convince the Emperor that they
have "magical" cloth only "the wise" can see. Not wanting to appear
unwise himself, he commissions these men to make him a suit of "magical" clothes fit for royalty. Here's where the story gets uncomfortable on
purpose: While the Emperor cannot see the cloth himself, he pretends
publicly that he can see it out of the fear of appearing "hopelessly stupid."
Making matters worse, his equally fearful servants follow suit by doing
the same. One bad decision after another follows as everyone moves for-

13

ward deluded and in denial. The painfully humiliating turning point is when "the new suit" is finished. The tailors pretend to dress the Emperor, attending to every delusional detail. Once finished, the Emperor pretends to don the suit and proudly marches in a parade before his subjects who energetically join in the fantasy. The dilemma is this: no one wants to admit that all they could really see was a half-naked ruler in his boxer shorts. Finally, one member of the crowd still connected to reality, one too young to engage in adult deception shouts out: "The Emperor has no clothes!" The Emperor cringes, suspecting the assertion is true, but holds himself up proudly and *continues the procession*.

Appearance collides with reality.

When it comes to the topic of men, the church is playing Andersen's Emperor role perfectly—it is hoping that unpleasant and uncomfortable realities about itself will remain unacknowledged while deep within it knows the assertion being made about its men is true. Painfully but proudly, the church continues a procession of appearances. The appearance of church health. The appearance of successful weekend services. The appearance of various and widespread small groups. The appearance of discipleship programs. The appearance of several different ministries and outreaches. The appearance of meaningful missions abroad. The appearance that all is well. All of these thinly veiled appearances mask a deep and abiding reality that is so obvious no one wants to say it out loud.

> The church continues a procession of appearances.

Why are there three times as many women in church as men? Why do the men gather in large numbers outside the church but not inside the church? Why do we have such a hard time finding good leaders for our ministries and groups? Why do we have a huge weekend attendance, but when we hold a men's event, we can't draw more than a handful? Why are so many marriages being ruined by pornography and affairs? Where are all the dads? Why aren't we more involved in the community? Why do we have so much trouble raising funds? Why doesn't the pastor champion strong men's programming, initiatives, and opportunities? After all, in most cases he's a man!

It stands to reason that painfully obvious things are, at times, the most difficult to bring up. This is especially true with leaders. It doesn't matter whether you are the head of a household, head of a Fortune 100 business, or the head of a local church. People closest to you rarely tell you the truth. Their reasons are many. You might sign their paycheck. You might pay the bills. You might react negatively toward them. You might get embarrassed, and they don't want to be the source of it. You might suffer from the "pedestal" effect where, because of your position of influence, your feet could *never* smell. You need to remain a friend versus become a potential enemy. For whatever reason the people close to you are not giving you some needed feedback, which, in the end, might provide the key to breaking through longstanding obstacles to success. What you are left with as a leader is a powerful delusion that all is well.

We all need someone to stand in our blind spot.

As for me, I am the boy in *The Emperor's New Clothes* who doesn't understand or care about keeping up appearances when I see something horribly confusing and obvious within the body of Christ. I see men in the audience of the church but not in the army. I see millions of affiliated men who can be activated powerfully. After twenty years of evangelizing and pastoring men, speaking into the lives of hundreds of thousands, personally conducting hundreds of conferences, training hundreds of churches, reading tens of thousands of evaluations from men, interviewing pastors all over the world, and receiving hundreds of e-mails from women, I have drawn a few inescapable and uncomfortable conclusions.

> We all need someone to stand in our blind spot.

- If the men of our churches are not healthy, then our churches are not healthy.
- If the men of our churches are affiliated but not activated toward helping the vision of the local church, we have an underutilized asset.

- If churches are reaching men poorly, they are delivering God's justice poorly in the cultures and communities where they are planted or being newly planted.
- If churches were intentionally investing in men, they would have a robust leadership engine and have to fund fewer professional staff.
- If churched men were activated versus just affiliated, church initiatives would be accelerated and achieved faster.
- If male involvement in the local church is weak, it is because our vision in the church for them is weak.
- If the church is unintentional with its men, it is permitting culture to shape the identities of its men, steal their energy, and shape their expression.
- If the church continues to attract women and children, it will *not attract men* or draw from diverse segments of society.
- If the church becomes a center of masculine transformation, it will attract multiple segments of society crossing gender, racial, intellectual, and economic lines.
- If the church does not deal with the issue of the invisibility of its men, it will remain painfully in denial and in poor health as the body of Christ.

> In place of intelligent and intentional men's community is a view that is dangerous and deceptive: the thought that knowledge alone will transform a man.

So what about that eight-hundred-pound gorilla in the room of our church family? Let's be sure about one thing for now: it's a *him*, not a her. Like the noble in Andersen's story who gets taken by a couple of con men, the church has been cleverly taken hostage when it comes to it's men, their role, and how to integrate them. Pastors intuitively sense the reality, urgency, and potency of male *leadership*, but they are at a loss for how to meaningfully evangelize and *equip them in a proactive way*. Pancake breakfast meetings, outdoor activities, sermon mentions, Father's Day blessings, and once-a-year conferences with no larger message to the men other than "this is something you should do" or "this will be good for you" does not stir the masculine soul. In place of intelligent and intentional men's community is a view that is dangerous and deceptive: the thought that knowledge alone will transform a man. As a consequence, men are treated like the quirky uncle in our spiritual family: invite and welcome him to special occasions but don't make him a stakeholder or, God forbid, critical to the success of the mission.

Faced with a pervading sense that connecting with men is just too hard, too much of a threat, or too chauvinistic to address aggressively, the men respond in kind. They are left to feel that their unique gifts and strengths as men are undervalued or not valued at all. They say to themselves:

- I am not really needed.
- They (the leadership at church) want to use my energy and resources but have no plan to help or develop me meaningfully *as a man*.
- I can't see where I fit into the plans here.
- I know where I am welcomed and fit in *outside* the church.
- They have got me, I am here, but they don't know what to do with me.
- I like the weekend messages well enough so I will attend.
- Leadership lip service but no meaningful action.

The result: men never move from the audience to the army of leaders who form ranks around their pastor and the vision God has called them to pursue in sufficient numbers. They affiliate but never activate. There is no perceived meaning or context for them to be or do more. How many times have you heard a senior pastor say to his men, "The vision God has given this church is way bigger than me, and I

> The result: men never move from the audience to the army of leaders who form ranks around the pastor.

am not going to be able to pull it off without your help and God's power." That's meaningful. No, instead, our men are forced to look to the broken male culture around them to validate their needs for significance and substance. Both the cost and the consequences of not moving men from the weekend structure into a strong secondary community and then into the leadership community of the local church is high, unnecessary, and tragic for the man and kingdom.

Above all, in one form or another, Satan wins.

Bleacher Guy

Affiliated. Attending. Listening. Leaving.

Do you know this man? His name at our church is Bleacher Guy. You see we have bleachers in our worship center that are located *way* in the back. The bleacher seats are as far away from the stage and pulpit as you can get. They are also immediately accessible when you walk in and provide an easier path to the exits. Bleacher Guy takes in the message from a large screen versus in person even though he is physically in the same room as the person speaking. He is in attendance but not present. He can leave unobstructed during the offering without the pastor seeing the whites of his eyes. He can fall asleep, doodle, and text message freely from the bleachers without fear. Bleacher Guy goes to church because his wife goes and his kids are involved in the youth program. He goes to church not because he "needs" it but because it appears the right thing to do. Maybe his boss or client attends too. As Bleacher Guy reads the environment, listens to all the announcements, experiences the worship music, sees the word "SHARE" or "BELONG" or "FELLOWSHIP" on a banner, he senses no masculine context or personal appeal. It is all generic and mostly feminine in his mind. The cross? Now *that* is manly. Everything else wears a skirt (or so he thinks).

Bleacher Guy is not just the affiliated attender but a metaphor for

> Do you know this man? His name at our church is Bleacher Guy.

the guy who is both relationally and emotionally distant from the vision of the church. The church has his presence but not his power. His career, outside pursuits, close friends, kids' activities, worldly appetites, or professional sports teams get his best ideas, energies, and expressions. He is present in the culture but not in the church. He's got mad skills and major mojo, but he has never been told directly that he is specifically needed at church *by anyone*. There is no intentional effort to meet, recruit, get to know, help, and call for him to be on the team. It's the elementary school playground all over again—no one likes to be picked last or not picked at all to join a team. Even more confusing is the fact that his Bible seems to be full of exploits and stories of great men who were dangerous with goodness, delivered God's justice, stuck it to evil, and sacrificed for a higher allegiance.

Where are those guys?

If only Bleacher Guy was that one-dimensional. In that case, all we would have to do is "de-girlify" the programs, preaching, and purposes of the church and inject it with a visible dose of testosterone. In reality Bleacher Guy is more like an iceberg. You only see the tip. Below the waterline of his life are a whole host of issues, insecurities, and emotions that make up the real substance of his existence and create much of the distance he puts between himself and the church. These "below the waterline" realities are exerting great emotional pressure and causing him to lose sleep, lose his moral compass, lose his cool, lose relationship, and lose confidence. His issues are powerful, personal, and man specific. More important, there is no forum for him to process these issues that doesn't force him to admit a weakness or failing by his mere attendance. Either he is a sex addict needing a meeting every week, or he is "normal" and doesn't need any help.

So Bleacher Guy is stuck in the mud (or his bleacher seat, if you prefer) knowing that he could be more than what he has

> He's got mad skills and major mojo, but he has never been told directly that he is specifically needed at church *by anyone*.

become. He's out there by the millions waiting for someone to give him an excuse to say "yes" to salvation and personal masculine transformation in the church context. He's hungry and not being fed. He's naked and no one is clothing him. He's an iceberg presenting the tip of his life while hiding the substance of his life. But that's not all. He's also a ten-megaton warhead the church can detonate in this hour to change the world. Help *him* get a win that means something to him and look out.

Meet Paul.

He is the original and actual Bleacher Guy where I got the character. Paul sat in the bleachers of Saddleback Church for seven years thinking all of the things, carrying around all the feelings, and fighting all the internal battles I just mentioned above for the most part. The tip of his iceberg looked like this: ex-college football player, successful pharmaceutical sales executive, smooth talker, trainer, strong, and in command. Below the waterline? Let's just say *a lot.* He was that all-too-common blend of outwardly confident and sure guy whose eyes betrayed his outer presentation. There was fear in his eyes about a lot of things his body language did not reveal. Fragmented family issues. Identity issues connected to being adopted. Acceptance issues. Career transitions. And powerful negative emotions connected to all of these. After Paul had spent seven years in the bleachers, Tom Crick (my partner for this book) asked him to come to our men's leadership community on Thursday mornings. The result?

Bleacher Guy exploded.

Paul encountered mentors, messages, and models that passed the "sniff" test his outer image required to keep coming back and that gave God the opportunity to get under the waterline of Paul's life. Slowly but surely God began to transform his fears into faith in a loving God who makes men secure enough to look beyond themselves. He caught God's vision for his life in the church context and under the church's vision for the community. His experience was so transforming, he wanted every next step toward true significance and leadership we could offer him. Today Paul is our men's director at one of our regional campuses and has led hundreds of men through the same process he experienced years earlier. Proof that it is never too late to become the man he should have been.

Bleacher guy. Pew sitter. Church potato. The eight-hundred-pound gorilla.

Call the "affiliated" Christian man in the church what you want, but we must activate him for the bride of Christ to be healthy, ready, and proud to meet her groom. And know this: Bleacher Guy is dying to move from the audience to the army, *helping you* reach, care for, train, and deploy many more men into the mission and vision of your local church.

The only question is: Will you see him the way God does?

Remember Jesus' words: *"For where your treasure is, there your heart will be also. The eye is the lamp of the body. If your eyes are healthy, your whole body will be full of light. But if your eyes are unhealthy, your whole body will be full of darkness. If then the light within you is darkness, how great is that darkness!" (Matt. 6:21–23).* The context of the passage is the investments we make and how that brings out our energies and passions. The Greek word for *healthy* here implies *generous,* and the word for *unhealthy* here implies *stingy.*

Let's use my "Paul" as an example. If the church sees and treasures Paul, it will come alongside and help him. It will invest in him. This is the equivalent of a healthy or generous outlook toward him. When that perception is right, Paul's energies invade our body and fill it with light or more health. The church's generosity toward helping men brings an equal and opposite reaction of generosity on the part of men toward the church. The opposite is also true. If the church sees but doesn't treasure Paul, it does not bother to come alongside him in meaningful ways. It doesn't invest in him. It's outlook is unhealthy. This stinginess in our approach to him breeds an unhealthy and reciprocal stinginess from him back into our Body. We lose his energy, lose his light, lose his transformational health, and multiply the perception among the rest of the men to remain in the audience versus the army.

> Call the "affiliated" Christian man in the church what you want, but we must activate him for the bride of Christ to be healthy, ready, and proud to meet her groom.

Bad for the man. Bad for the church. Great for the devil.

"What You Are Doing Is Not Good"

Moses was "the man."

Let's review: success over the most powerful man in the known world, led by the pillars of fire, and crossed the Red Sea. Not bad. Then we have the manna and the quail, the water from the rock, and his, literally, praying Israel to victory over the Amalekites to round out this eventful first season of service (Exod. 7–17). But now, safely removed from Pharaoh and relieved from the pressure of a war, Jethro comes to reconnect and reinvigorate his son-in-law Moses with a little family time. A grateful Moses has "Jethro therapy" and lets out everything he's been holding inside. All of the above and more spills out of this leader of leaders. Moses talks, Jethro listens, they fellowship, and they worship together as men. It is an awesome snapshot of what all of God's shepherds need: a safe harbor in the form of another man who understands and affirms him in the midst of the pressures of leading God's people.

Day two is a different story.

Jethro shadows and observes Moses minister, lead, and care for the people. But instead of celebrating, he's watching and calculating how much longer his son-in law will enjoy success. His conclusion? Not long. When all the other men around Moses either wouldn't or couldn't see it or say it, Jethro tells Moses what he most probably already suspects is true but can't admit or fix without some encouragement. Watch Jethro expose the eight-hundred-pound gorilla.

> *What you are doing is not good.* You and these people who come to you will only wear yourselves out. The work is too heavy for you; you cannot handle it alone. Listen now to me and I will give you some advice, and may God be with you. You must be the people's representative before God and bring their disputes to him. Teach them his decrees and instructions, and show them the way they are to live and how they are to behave. But select capable men from all the people—men who fear God, trustworthy men who hate

dishonest gain—and appoint them as officials over thousands, hundreds, fifties and tens. Have them serve as judges for the people at all times, but have them bring every difficult case to you; the simple cases they can decide themselves. That will make your load lighter, because they will share it with you. If you do this and God so commands, you will be able to stand the strain, and all these people will go home satisfied. (Exod. 18:17–23, italics mine)

The community of faith had a leader. But that community was breaking down unnecessarily (getting too heavy to take care of). In the community of faith, there were men that were ready and called by God to help who were not activated by their leader either by choice, by ego, or by sheer ignorance. Whatever the case, *God wanted these guys in the game.* So in love, Jethro has the man-to-man with Moses. He delivers what initially must have felt like bad news so that there can be a healthier future for the leader, the people, and the plan of God. In the end, Moses receives it not as a stab to kill but a cut to heal. Jethro puts his son-in-law's ministry on the grinding wheel, Moses weathers the sparks and friction, the leader comes out sharper, and the blade of his leadership slices through the thick needs of the people with precision and ease. Iron sharpens iron.

> In the community of faith, there were men that were ready and called by God to help.

Moses listened to his father-in-law and did everything he said. He chose capable men from all Israel and made them leaders of the people, officials over thousands, hundreds, fifties and tens. They served as judges for the people at all times. The difficult cases they brought to Moses, but the simple ones they decided themselves. (Exod. 18:24–26)

Jethro saw the man, and the man was failing in his charge *unnecessarily.* All the muscle Moses needed for the mission was right under his nose. This snapshot on spiritual movement, leadership, and God's pat-

> Is it possible to have a healthy church without healthy men?

tern for getting it done was taken by God and displayed in Scripture for us to see an unhealthy pattern, see God's plan of correction, and imitate Moses' response with our own communities of faith. It is a prophetic whack on the head for all of us who have responded to God's call to lead God's people. We cannot do it alone, and we are to raise up men out of our own house to meet the needs of the people. We will dive more deeply into this topic and see this pattern repeated in every age of biblical leadership in Section II.

For now let me just say, I see the church all over the world struggling unnecessarily to deliver its mission. I see churches pouring massive amounts of resources into initiatives and staff unnecessarily because they lack a network of men who could easily achieve those same ends if they were commissioned and equipped the right way. I see churches praying to expand their influence evangelistically in their communities, bring justice to women and children, transform lives, and fulfill the Great Commission and Great Commandment. I also see that God has answered these prayers, and they are sitting in the pews, bleachers, and periphery of our churches. He has given you the men.

> All the muscle Moses needed for the mission was right under his nose.

God is calling the church to move them from the audience to the army.

Key Learnings

- Not having the perspective of another point of view creates a limiting and often disastrous perspective of reality.
- Aggressive transparency and integrity must be cultivated by leadership when the mission is stalled or the needs of those we lead are not getting met adequately.
- Honest feedback from Scripture and the Body, not codependency

with church fads or culture, should power our approaches and initiatives.

- God's glory and power reside in truth and reality, not denial and fantasy over church issues.
- The goal is to have healthier leaders and healthier churches through activating the affiliated.
- Events, activities, and programs most often leave no substantial effect on raising leadership. Proximity to these does not transform a man.
- Leadership lip service does not activate.
- Where the church does not activate culture most certainly will.
- Men *already present* in our congregation are the gold underneath the floorboards of the church.

Chapter 3

Dealing Aces
to the Devil

*"So I will go to the leaders and speak to them; surely
they know the way of the LORD, the requirements of
their God. But with one accord they too had broken off
the yoke and torn off the bonds. Therefore a lion from
the forest will attack them, a wolf from the desert will
ravage them, a leopard will lie in wait near their towns
to tear to pieces any who venture out, for their rebellion
is great and their backslidings many."*

JEREMIAH 5:5–6

A high-value target.

This is what a sniper sees nestled in the crosshairs of his high-precision rifle. When I read the book *Point of Impact* by Stephen Hunter, I was immersed into the world of the sniper for the first time. Many things about the story appealed to me as a man, war buff, and novel reader, but many *more things struck me as a pastor!* More specifically, the whole idea of a sniper's reducing the enemy's fighting ability by striking at high-value targets (especially officers) and in the process pinning down and demoralizing your enemy. The goal is: *maximum disruption to enemy operations.* Did you hear that, pastor?

Target leaders. Pin down. Demoralize. Disrupt operations.

Some other aspects that struck me personally as a leader of men in the church were:

- A sniper will select and shoot his targets in descending order by rank.
- A sniper will identify targets by observing behavior which suggests that others depend on him, defer to him, and react to his presence in groups.
- A sniper works hard to find the right "hide site" or concealed position that gives him the widest view, best camouflage, and clearest line of sight to the target.
- A good sniper has profound psychological effect on the enemy by inducing constant stress in opposing forces that accompanies the elimination of leadership and the inability to locate the source of disruption.
- A sniper's dream is when his enemy lies down and waits when targeted by him. Doing this allows him to pick off the men one after another. "Get down!" is music to his ears.
- A sniper usually aims at the chest because he depends on maximum tissue damage, organ trauma, and blood loss to make the kill.

So let's review. He lies in wait. He patiently anticipates and hopes for that moment when the high-value target is isolated and separated. He closes in. He settles his aim. His finger moves to the trigger. He takes a deep breath.

Gone.

Another leader and all the knowledge and influence he commanded—gone.

Acceptable Losses?

He starts at the top.

For a sniper, rank is synonymous with influence. And when it comes to our topic of the church, men, and their capacity to deliver help or harm, Satan is no fool. In fact, the Bible, from this perspective, chronicles a savvy enemy, lying in wait specifically for men, capitalizing on their ignorance of his proximity and presence to take them down. In the process the man is neutralized, people around him suffer, and the church's best potential leaders are carried away from God's purposes, conformed to a pattern of broken male culture in the world, or both. In the most basic analysis, one can assign potential power in the church by simply recognizing who the devil is stalking and killing. Not surprisingly the reality that men in massive numbers are being neutralized shock no one today. What *is shocking* is the willingness of churches to act like men in the community and men in the church are *acceptable losses*.

> In the most basic analysis, one can assign potential power in the church by simply recognizing who the devil is stalking and killing.

Both Satan and God's leaders should share this keen interest in men. Listen to the prophetic words of Jeremiah strike deep into the issue of men, leaders, *and* their value both to God's leaders and God's enemy:

> So I will go to the leaders and speak to them; surely they know the way of the LORD, the requirements of their God. But with one accord they too had broken off the yoke and torn off the bonds. Therefore a lion from the forest will attack them, a wolf from the desert will ravage them, a leopard will lie in wait near their towns to tear to pieces any who venture out, for their rebellion is great and their backslidings many. (Jer. 5:5–6)

Can you imagine Jeremiah's disappointment? Not only had the men in the community of faith been targeted and taken down but so had their leaders: *"But with one accord they too had broken off the yoke and torn off the bonds."* Men in the community were wooed and drawn into the slimy pits of the godless male culture around them, which was unsettling to the man of God. But to make matters worse, the leadership, the shepherds themselves, had broken free of their spiritual identity and duties connected to their positions as well. As a seasoned spiritual combat veteran, Jeremiah knows there is only one outcome: a massacre for God's people. It's the spiritual equivalent of the killing fields—bones everywhere. Just the remains testify of men once fully alive in God. No wonder they call him the weeping prophet. At the edge of a spiritual abyss, God's man sent to bring spiritual health is staring into a gigantic male leadership vacuum which guarantees one thing: suffering.

A church's attitude about men reflects its ministry to men.

Satan wisely sees that men are leaders, influencers, and game-changing assets in the kingdom battle. He devotes massive resources to culturally lure, recruit, and use men to execute his evil plans in the world. He even thought he could win over the Son of God. He plans, plots, and consistently seeks to control the heart of every man on Earth. Do you believe that? The church, by contrast, unwisely sees men as the reserve players with a limited role in the big picture. It allocates little if any direct resources to reach the unsaved man trapped in the cords of culture or to directly and meaningfully equip

> A church's attitude about men reflects its ministry to men.

the saved in our ranks. It sponsors events. Satan prizes winning the heart of a man and incarnating the spirit of the world through him to bring destruction and death to those around him. He is central. By contrast, the Christian church simply laments and accepts that it is woefully out of balance in how its women practically and statistically outperform its men in every category of spiritual life and discipline (a problem, incidentally, not present in Hinduism, Judaism, and Islam).

The devil has it down to a science.

Our sniper has rested comfortably in the same "hide site" for centuries, camouflaged in culture, neutralizing the potentially powerful spiritual identities of men with powerful "isms" promising man-specific validation apart from Christ (i.e., materialism, hedonism, narcissism, intellectualism, atheism, tribalism, communism, fascism, relativism, syncretism, mysticism, humanism, etc.). Jesus warned His men directly of this trap, telling them point-blank: "If you belonged to the world [culture], it would love you as its own. As it is you do not belong to the world [culture] but I have chosen you out of the world [culture]. That is why the world [culture] hates you" (John 15:19, bracketed words are mine).

Jesus openly warns about the threat, which begs certain questions. What's the church saying about the tempting world of broken male culture? Are we outing the devil as the sponsor of cultural masculinity? Are we showing men how cultural ways of believing and behaving are shallow substitutes for authentic manhood? Are we exposing their lack of merit and highlighting their chief export of selfishness and suffering? Are we telling men directly that Christlikeness is the apex expression of the just, strong, honorable, powerful, and caring man we all dreamed of being when we were little boys?

Too direct?

To this end Satan has enjoyed the withering psychological effect, dysfunction, and constant stress his targeted investment in men puts on the church. He relishes its attempts at forceful kingdom advance with the majority of its most capable warriors in the audience and not in the army. He loves the frustration of no gains. We appear to be enjoying it too because the church continues to deal the aces in its deck over to the devil.

Must feel good for him.

Think about it. Have you ever played cards, needed a certain card, and then got dealt the exact card you needed to win? It triggers joy on the inside. Hopefully you are able to keep your poker face and not overreact on the outside. Feelings of relief, excitement, satisfaction, and confidence flow because you are sure the card you've just been dealt will secure your victory and deflate the hopes of everyone else. Now imagine that over the course of a high-stakes game you keep being dealt the right cards, hand after hand, and you keep winning hand after hand. Something happens. Your confidence grows, you risk higher stakes, and you stay in this game as long as possible. In gambler's language you are "feeling it." So what does gambling, dealing aces, and "feeling it" have to do with the church right now at this time in history?

Everything.

> The church's ignorance is the devil's bliss.

When it comes to this discussion of men—saved and unsaved—Satan's gambling aggressively on a church that continues to deal him aces. And like a naïve poker player who is at the table with a seasoned gambler, the church unwittingly and continuously is "playing right into his hand." By not targeting unsaved men as central to their evangelistic strategies and by not providing saved men a meaningful vision of growth and involvement in the larger success and mission, we are turning over our strongest cards in the deck to an enemy that will gladly take the aces we are discarding like deuces.

The church's ignorance is the Devil's bliss.

> Therefore my people will go into exile for lack of understanding; those of high rank will die of hunger and the common people will be parched with thirst. Therefore Death expands its jaws, opening wide its mouth; into it will descend their nobles and masses with all their brawlers and revelers. (Isa. 5:13–14)

The context of these words is frighteningly specific concerning the "men of Judah" (5:5) and the broken male culture surrounding the men. Satanically sponsored cultural expressions of masculinity were successfully infecting and taking over the souls of God's men with disastrous consequences for *everybody*. God was looking for righteousness and justice but found the "isms" ruling the identities and priorities among his men. There was no noticeable difference anymore from a *character* perspective between God's men and the cultural man. This character transformation led to a *conduct* pandemic producing an enormous blast zone of suffering. Note the target: "Those of high rank" (aka men). Note the consequences: complete emotional and spiritual starvation of the people connected to these leaders as well as a comprehensive cultural absorption of the entire faith community by culture. *"Therefore Death expands its jaws, opening wide its mouth; into it will descend their nobles and masses with all their brawlers and revelers."* Satan wanted, targeted, tempted,

> If only the church prized men the way the devil does.

and took the aces that were dealt to him by God's people. It's a picture of swallowing a people whole.

If only the church prized men the way the devil does.

The Pound-for-Pound Church

Greatness must involve victory over quality opposition or significant odds.

In the boxing world I have just described Manny Pacquiao. You don't even have to love boxing to admire and respect this little man who packs a mighty punch. Manny Pacquiao has been appropriately labeled by fans of the sport, bloggers, sportswriters, and fellow boxers as the best "pound-for-pound" fighter in the modern era. In other words, as a boxer who has won titles in eight lighter weight divisions, he is *never* going to fight for the heavyweight championship of the world. That's because he is five feet six inches and weighs in at 150 pounds all wet in his street clothes. He is not going to be remembered like Muhammad Ali because his greatness in the sport is measured in different dimensions. These include: how many weight divisions he has won, the quality of his opponents, and his skills in the ring. I will never forget witnessing those skills for the first time. Hand speed. Power. Work rate. All masterful. You know a guy is great when you feel sorry for *everyone* he fights. In this way a pound-for-pound fighter designation gives you the greater measure of the boxer.

"Pound-for-pound" reflects that you are substantially more than what people see.

As pastors and members we easily confuse the measure of greatness in the local church. We all know and admire the heavyweights whose numbers are the size of small- to medium-size cities. (I should know because I am in one of those churches.) But one thing my senior pastor has taught me is not to elevate numbers beyond other dimensions of measurement God considers more important. He knows and I know that numbers do not translate to church health, disciple making, and God's justice being delivered missionally through our efforts. We also know that the scale of our church demands proportional measures of faith and fruitfulness with the people we have. We might be in the "heavyweight" division, but measured on the "pound-for-pound scale," we have found churches a fraction of our size outperforming us in many ways in areas of our weakness. Even on the "man scale" we have a long way to go to catch up proportionally to our "weight class" in men's ministry. But as we progress step-by-step, I see some of the other measures trending upward like men discipled and deployed, leaders placed into ministry, church health, family health, community involvement, personal evangelism, and justice being delivered to women and children.

> God weighs churches pound for pound, *not* seat for seat.

God weighs churches pound for pound *not seat for seat.*

A great pound-for-pound category is the quality of your efforts with men in the community and men in the church. More specifically, how are you doing in the battle to combat the devil's assault on the men God has called you to reach in your culture, community, congregation, or country? The devil can't stand a church or pastor who stops dealing him the aces he needs to deliver his diabolical schemes. In fact, he fears the church that starts delivering disciples who become great pound-for-pound God's men. These men are not just good attenders but also great activators of God's purposes in and through their lives. And while Satan can hijack one gender as easily as the other, he chooses to focus his efforts on the hearts of men for pure performance reasons. We must get this *precisely* because Satan does. He's showing his hand to us!

> While Satan can hijack one gender as easily as the other, he chooses to focus his efforts on the hearts of men for pure performance reasons.

Romans 5:19 puts the "pound-for-pound" strength and dimension regarding men in perspective for us like no other verse of the Bible. *"For just as through the disobedience of the one man the many were made sinners, so also through the obedience of the one man the many will be made righteous."* Did you see it? One man impacting many. One blast zone produces death. The other blast zone produces life. Satan believes in and knows the impact and appreciates the power of "one man." Adam listened and death reigned. Jesus did not bite on Satan's suggestions and life reigns forever. Men will be in Adam, or they will be in Christ. He loves and uses the one type and deeply fears

> A church overweight with numbers but short on healthy men is not a good pound-for-pound church.

and loathes the other type. More than any one of God's creatures, he understands that human history itself rises and falls on the shoulders of men. Men are both the thrill of his victories *and* the agony of his defeats.

But do we believe this like he obviously does?

A church overweight with numbers but short on healthy men is not a good pound-for-pound church. A church with big events for men that is producing small numbers of leaders is not a good pound-for-pound church. A church that is investing in social justice outreaches without investing in reaching the men causing the problems is not a good pound for pound church. A church that measures itself by weekend attendance over the raising up of leaders and sending of its men into ministries is not a good pound-for-pound church. A church that does not recognize that if you appeal to women you don't reach men but if you appeal to the man you reach both is not a good pound-for-pound church. A church that puts its young boys with female leaders without the influence of other male leaders to model healthy male character is not a good pound-for-pound church. Pastors that are functionally disconnected from the network of men in their church, isolating themselves from the very men they need to pull off big visions are not good pound-for-pound pastors.

It's all-out war.

Satan is focused on keeping men leery of church and keeping the church ambivalent about men. That's a huge victory for evil's enterprising leader. Conversely, if your church sees and prizes men the way Satan does, moves intentionally to balance out other strengths with a strong men's culture, and becomes good at winning new men to Christ, you may consider that a hard-won victory *over* Satan. More important, the spoils of turning the tide in *that* war will bring supernatural blessing and power into your efforts. My friend Dave Murrow, author of *Why Men Hate Going to Church,* has often said that men are like Miracle-Gro (the super plant food) for churches: "Sprinkle them throughout your efforts, and your church will grow." I couldn't agree more. Pound for pound your giving will grow, your church health will grow, your church unity will grow, you will keep more youth longer, and you will have more leaders to drive initiatives and fewer critics! The men in your community and in your congregation are high-value targets. If you don't make them a priority, Satan will. If you don't have a plan, Satan does. If you don't win him to Christ, Satan will win him over to the culture.

No more kill shots.

Key Learnings

- We must consistently be on the lookout for Satan's disruptive devices. The primary targets are unsuspecting and complacent men and men's leadership.
- Lack of male leadership in the church almost certainly guarantees an environment for human suffering to grow like bacteria in a petri dish.
- Where the church is complacent about winning the hearts of men, Satan is working diligently and happy to receive the gift to use for his purposes.
- When the church is satisfied with male presence without activation toward a culture of Christ, Satan gains valuable ground.
- There is little discernible difference between cultural man and God's man in our cultures today.
- A church that does not heavily invest in developing the spiritual leadership of it's men will produce a men's culture of spiritual bystanders.

Chapter 4

One Men's Movement

*The eye cannot say to the hand, "I don't need you!" And
the head cannot say to the feet, "I don't need you!"*

1 Corinthians 12:21 niv

October 4, 1997—Washington, DC

I was there.

More than one million men were on their knees in total silence asking for God's hand to move upon our nation. Not a mouth dared utter a word and ruin the call to prayer. It was so quiet I could hear the wind blowing across an ocean of men who were facedown, searching their souls. There was so much faith and dedication to Jesus on the table in that moment, such humility and palpable repentance, it felt like the sky was going to rip open. This moment was swallowing all doubt, all fear, all rejection, all loneliness, all temptation, all struggle, all mistakes, all regrets, all selfishness, and countless other maladies of earth while at the same time replacing each with the faith, hope, and love of a Father. Sons of all cultures were now sons of Christ, in God's lap, enjoying a moment of grace and listening to the Spirit of truth minister powerfully in the inner man. Many of you reading these words were there too. Those who weren't can appreciate the scale and scope of a genuine move of the Holy Spirit like this. God's men did stand in the gap that day, and in that particular moment it became a sacred assembly of men for all present. Moments like these are rare, special, powerful, life changing, and glorifying to God.

They are also problematic for the church.

I have talked to pastors around the globe about the respective movements in their countries from Mighty Men in South Africa to Promise Keepers in America to Christian Vision for Men in the U.K. The common denominator with all of these visions, gatherings, movements and the associated events, where men are momentarily inspired and activated, is that they are not sustainable without the energy, support, network, and vision of the local church. Study them closely, and each of them struggles to layer their vision and mission onto the vision and mission of the local church. No matter how well intentioned, articulated, and planned, the idea that movements started as reactions to what the church was not providing men, then asking for its men and partnership, feels as disingenuous as it looks. And yet I remember being commissioned as a participant in the movement to "bring this energy, enthusiasm, and engagement back home to your local church and stay connected."

So were hundreds of thousands of other men just like me.

I can speak confidently to these phenomena because I was right in the middle of it all as an enthusiastic attender, then later as a men's pastor and platform speaker. Imagine my amazement hearing leaders of parachurch movements talk of pastors in the church as "the obstacle" right in front of me and offer seminars on how to "Win Over Your Pastor to the Movement." These are godly men and dear friends with amazing hearts, but even the most saintly of men get frustrated. And they did—with the church and with pastors who weren't respecting the reality that these parachurch men's events were commanding the very audience the church had seemingly lost: the men. We are talking titanic numbers of men, national events, huge press and recognition, publishing movements, and major endorsements—all this and the hearts of their own male congregation members. One would think the church would adjust its mission and structure to affirm what was happening. Right?

Wrong.

While these events enjoy modest to openly affirming recognition publicly by many pastors, adoption of the movement into the church family could be classified only as marginal at best. As both a participant and a pastor, two things struck me. First, what was the church's response to all of this masculine activity and investment occurring outside its walls, in stadiums, large arenas, coffee shops, garages, country farms, and remote ranches? More specifically, why didn't the church, upon seeing vast numbers of its men getting excited about Christ, ask itself: *What is going on that is so attractive and strong for the men that we are apparently not offering?* Or how about simply observing, *Wow. We could sure use some of that energy and enthusiasm here!* Then, perhaps after giving it some thought, going about the process of developing meaningful ways to engage and equip men *in the church.*

Seems so normal to ask those types of questions and take some steps in that direction, doesn't it? And yet we did not see an increase in the hiring of men's pastors; we did not see seminaries offer classes on reaching or training men, and we didn't see any significant adjustment in the way the church handled men's ministry. It was content to be largely ambivalent internally while not daring to disparage the movement. To say this reaction—or better, lack of intelligent reaction—was, and still is, a huge mistake on the part of pastors would be understating the obvious. In hindsight, I believe God was showing the church what could be and provided a clear X-ray for the world to see the broken bone in the body of Christ.

Up on the screen was an ugly fracture of the "man-bone" of the body.

These parachurch men's movements were high-definition *signs* glowing in plain sight for the whole world to see the power, hope, strength, unity, faith, and willingness of men to repent and renew their faith in Jesus. It was a vision of healing for the compound fracture among men in the body of Christ. In response the local

> Up on the screen was an ugly fracture of the "man-bone" of the body.

church yawned and went on with business as usual for the most part. Weekend services, children's ministries, student ministries, and other missions were resumed while the men who attended these events along with their enthusiasm for God were left without a viable, ongoing place or platform to continue the process in the local church. Most men would have to wait for 365 days until next year's big event came back into town. It took on a circus-type atmosphere. Each time the circus came to town, the tents went up, the tents were filled, signs and wonders unfolded, men were gripped by the Holy Spirit, and then the tents were folded up as fast as they were put up while the men begged for one more song. And once the last note was sung and the final benediction was given, excited but orphaned men were left with the hopeless task of reproducing such a meaningful connection on a local level.

To the credit of the parachurch ministries, massive resources and personnel were devoted to contacting local churches seeking to come alongside and help them develop their men's ministries. Many took the call but comparably few "adopted." Adopted ministries do not fair well among the naturally birthed and homegrown ministries of local churches. It had the feel of an outsider. Even denominationally sponsored men's efforts failed to hit the mark because local pastors felt they did not pass the "sniff" test for a locally owned and operated initiative. How do I know? I witnessed it firsthand in my own church! It didn't stick.

Now let's flip it.

The second dynamic that struck me relates to the millions of men impacted by these gatherings positively and their approach upon coming back to their local churches. More specifically, the gross misinterpretation of the metrics (numbers participating) for a mandate to muscle the church to adopt the movement as its own. The unmistakable perception was that numbers were synonymous with God's anointing and a mandate right? Apparently not. Because when local pastors in congregations of every size didn't open up their wallets, change their infrastructure, and adopt a new mission and vision built around their men's community, the response ranged from shock and awe to anger. For a while cooperation with the local church, while attractive, was not necessary because the momentum and metrics were dizzying (and blinding).

And as time wore on and men's movements needed a vision that was bigger than "men are gathering again," the church became increasingly important for survival. The sobering fact of the matter was that for the other 364 nonevent days these men were members of local churches. This realization combined with the lack of a transcendent vision, caused the solid rocket boosters to fall off these movements. The result? Comfort turned to concern, and then concern turned to panic in the span of a few short years. Officially or unofficially, churches and pastors became the obstacle the movement had to conquer to survive. And just as the church failed to ask the right questions to learn and possibly become stronger, the parachurch men's movement and its ambassadors failed to ask local pastors some simple questions too. Ones that show you truly have *the pastors' interests* in mind.

- What are the core values and vision of *your* church?
- What has God called you to do here in *your* community?
- What initiatives do you have that need energy and muscle?
- How can the men of our church help support what God has called *you* to do?
- Where is leadership most desperately needed?
- Would you be open to getting men connected, healthy, strong, and going into those areas of need?

Sometimes the solution *is* the approach.

Just say the word *fizzle* and you will understand how this relationship ended up panning out between parachurch men's movements and the local church. While what I have just said is a generalization and not true in every instance (like Promise Keepers Canada, for example), we have to know where this relationship has been in order to chart a new course for where it is going. I can speak to this because I was "in it" up to my neck on both the church side as a pastor and the men's movement side as a speaker and consultant. Some of my good friends were leading the parachurch men's movement in America,

> Sometimes the solution *is* the approach.

and much of my insight comes from *their hindsight* after reflecting on what went right and wrong. Pain provides clarity.

Pain can also produce a new vision.

The Power of Neglect

Acceptance. Affirmation. Validation.

Every man seeks it, wants it, craves it, and attaches to those who provide it. Give millions of men who feel unvalidated, unneeded, and undervalued an outlet or context to *get validated* and you have got a powerful recipe for an explosive movement. Throughout recorded history revolutions and uprisings of all kinds have been spawned by the power of neglect lying just underneath the surfaces of nations, nationalities, and names of guys like Vladimir, Adolf, and Osama who recognize and exploit how to use that power for evil. Other men with names like Abraham (Lincoln), Martin (Luther and King), Billy (Graham), and "Coach" had divine visions rooted in the same power but used the dynamic for good and for God. The common denominator is the deep-rooted desire burning in the hearts of men to be someone great and to do something great. In the New Testament we see this in Jesus' own disciples jockeying for significance as they feel a "movement" coming on, led by the wise and powerful leader from Nazareth. Jesus smartly doesn't discourage this masculine need or downplay the desire for validation or greatness; He simply reframes it, redefines it, and redeploys these desires for the kingdom. There are no standards to conform or measure up to, only a strong, personal calling to authentic manhood He knows is pregnant inside of the men just waiting to be tapped. Let's watch the film.

> Pain provides clarity. Pain can also produce a new vision.

Jesus called them together and said, "You know that those who are regarded as rulers of the Gentiles lord it over them, and their high officials exercise authority over them. Not so with you. Instead, whoever wants to become great among you must be your servant, and whoever wants to be first must be slave of all. For even the Son of Man did not come to be served, but to serve, and to give his life as a ransom for many." (Mark 10:42–45)

For better or for worse, giving men the opportunity to be great produces sacrificial disciples as well as suicide bombers. Purpose, transcendence, meaning, legacy, and eternity wrapped in a strong purpose will always attract men. Causes like this enable men to win the identities, energies, and expressions of whole cultures in large numbers. Causes that are perceived to be weaker will be bled dry of their men by other movements, philosophies, and cultural phenomena that are strong. So what do men pregnant with desires for greatness, Jesus tapping into that desire, the power of neglect, and morphing the modern men's movement into a worldwide giant have to do with your church?

Everything.

When the church does not recognize the power of validation among men and its evil twin called the power of neglect, it has effectively forfeited its men to other cultural movements, Christian and non-Christian, *that do* recognize and resource this need in men. As pastors we should be grateful that parachurch men's movements made the gospel, salvation, and transformation central to their messages and movements. We should be grateful that the men leading them were obedient to God, diligent in their season, and determined to be faithful. Millions were won to Christ

> For better or for worse, giving men the opportunity to be great produces sacrificial disciples as well as suicide bombers

but millions were also orphaned because the church responded unwisely and insecurely. We adopted a cynical and fearful approach instead of dialoguing, working together, and matching strengths so that the vision of the local church was accelerated. But there is another cold, hard fact that we must face as pastors that is even less pleasant to swallow.

Our men were naturally drawn to what *we failed to provide.*

Thank God so many went toward Christ-centered spiritual movements and leaders who loved God versus toward synthetic and cultural men's movements sponsored by evil. These global parachurch movements were *not* intended to carry or replace the church's responsibility to disciple and equip it's own men. God did, however, use these movements to provide what I would call "foster care" of His men, a safe harbor to pour out their desire for spiritual greatness while, at the same time, offer a stunning rebuke to the church for neglecting to shepherd its own men with care and concern.

Lesson learned?

Whether or not the local church has learned its lesson on this front is uncertain. What is certain is that the season of parachurch men's movements *showing the church the need* is over and the advent of church responsibility for its men is upon us. Notice what I *didn't say.* I didn't say the need for parachurch men's ministries is over. Far from it. Many of these ministries have developed tremendous skills at gathering men and providing powerful encounters which God wants to continue to use to bless large numbers of men in the local church. For example, while writing this book, I was in South Africa talking to a pastor about the parachurch men's movement called Mighty Men, founded and driven by a farmer named Angus Buchan (www.karoommc.co.za). It is an incredible story of a simple man being used by God in his country to show the church what men need and want. At one of his Mighty Men rallies, more than a quarter of a million men flocked to Angus's farm, pitched tents, worshipped God, and were blessed. As the pastor and I talked about Mighty Men and this event in particular, I said, "If I were you, I would use an event like that to bring my men but come to it with an intentional

> What is certain is that the season of parachurch men's movements *showing the church the need* is over and the advent of church responsibility for its men is upon us.

mission to use it to connect men into *ongoing groups and pathways meeting back at home.*" I took out a notepad and talked about the strategy I would use at a gathering like this, setting aside time for the men of our church to break into discussion groups with leaders to process what God was saying to them through the course of the event. These discussion groups would bond, talk, pray, and meet several times. I told the pastor I would place a leader of my choosing over each discussion group and task him with getting to know the men assigned to his discussion group. These leaders would then set a time for the group to continue to meet back at home and start the church's leader development pathway. It had never dawned on him *that he could use one movement to spawn another in his own church.* He thought: *All the energy and solidarity of an awesome gathering of men intentionally used to connect guys to a process in my own church providing me with leaders? I would love that!*

It's called matching strengths.

That said, there is a huge lesson being learned by all ministries to men spawned outside the church that need the energy, attendance, and resources of the men of the church to succeed. That is, they need to serve the local pastor, the local vision, and the local mission of the local church.

God's Woman

The church is God's woman.

It doesn't matter whether *you think* she is pretty, fat, or dumb. She's His. She's always first. She is the one Jesus is coming for. She is to be readied for His return. She carries His hopes and affections. She is the object of His gaze. She is a vast network of bodies of believers being led and equipped by overworked shepherds and lay volunteers whose small task is to meet the spiritual needs of 2.1 billion followers worldwide and fulfill the Great Commission. She looks like bodies of believers and budding preachers, contemporary music and contentious gossips, and leadership that ranges from the exceptional to the inept. She stumbles at times to be relevant. She lags behind the times in her appearance to the outside world. She seems unprofessional and undereducated in her approach at times too.

She has both the hypocrite and the hyperreligious in her ranks. And don't forget she is full of broken people healing from the effect of Adam's slip and fall from which none of us are fully recovered in this life.

That disturbing reality, along with her other imperfections, causes many men to abandon her for a self-styled pursuit of what she appears to be lacking. It also has spawned movements, models, and messengers which were reactions to needs she was not meeting at any given time. And while used by God for many purposes and providential plans, the presence and existence of these men or movements were never meant to replace *her*. We see this dynamic throughout church history both within and outside the church. She (the local church) remains the holder of His vision. To this end men's movements never "died"; they simply were not holders of the vision and the movements along with their men always go back to its owner.

This is the stone that has broken the back of movements spawned as reactions to what she (the church) has lacked, as well being the rod which has chastised reform movements that try to make her one dimensional from within. The church is a mysteriously powerful woman that has mystified and frustrated all hijackers from within and without. This reality eats away at organizations and movements that forget their purpose is to make the bride beautiful versus make themselves visible. Mixed motives masquerading as righteous missions litter the road to greatness for many men who deign to challenge this truth and their movements. This is certainly the tale of many men's ministries and movements that begin as reactions to what is lacking in the church and then, in a poetic irony, come back to the same churches they emotionally abandoned, to "help her" reach men.

How do I know this is true? Because I receive requests on a weekly basis to endorse or work with men and organizations committed to helping men who want me to use their materials in our church. But when I ask these same men seeking my endorsement and dollar if they are personally serving their local church and pastor with their energy and resources, an awkward silence falls over the conversation. Not all, but the vast majority are *not* using their passion and skill to serve their local pastor, rallying the men of his church behind their leader and driver of the vision. My message to all of us serving men is this: there is only one men's movement and "she" is the proven keeper.

Serve her.

The local church is the hope of the world, and the hope of the local church in this hour is her men. In other words the church has robust numbers of women and children, but there must be more. Missiologists, sociologists, and church statisticians will confirm this reality numerically and functionally. The emotional heart of the church (aka it's women) is beating strong while the New Testament power and aggression of its men are absent, needed, and being called on by the Holy Spirit for God's purposes *right now*.

> The local church is the hope of the world, and the hope of the local church in this hour is her men.

To my fellow pastors: Don't fear energetic, talented, or selfishly passionate men in your community. Under the control of the Holy Spirit, they will be your best leaders! Win them to Christ by offering them a strong moral and spiritual alternative to the shallow cultural vision. Similarly, don't fear excited men in the Lord. Yes, they are a bit unwieldy, but if you tell them you need them, have a clear path to be great in the church context and a process to take them there, they will respond! Lastly, don't be afraid of parachurch men's events. Use them to inspire, connect, and draw men into the nets of your *local* ongoing process.

Your movement has arrived.

As we consider engaging men in the community and men in the congregation in an intentional and intelligent way, our strongest motivator is seeing God's pattern of spiritual movement along these lines in both testaments. Over the next four chapters we are going to reflect on God, His chosen leaders, their missions, and how they accomplished them. We will track God's leaders from Abraham all the way to the apostle Paul. As we do, you are going to witness an amazing consistency and character to His strategy of movement in both Old and New Testaments. As the pattern of God's interaction with His leaders and the process of movement emerges, we want to pause and reflect as Scripture encourages: *"These things happened to them as examples and were written down as warnings for us, on whom the culmination of the ages has come" (1 Cor. 10:11).* That means we must see the pattern, study the pattern, and be responsible to apply the lessons that become visible as a *current* leader of God's people "on whom the culmination of the ages has come."

What will you see?

1. You will see God's pattern of using men as His chosen agents of influence.
2. You will see God's pattern of using men to lead movements He sponsors.
3. You will see God's pattern of supporting His leaders with an infrastructure of men.
4. You will see God's pattern of achieving health in the community of faith by addressing the hearts of the men.
5. You will see a pattern of God's leaders using the men God gave them to achieve the vision He planted in them.

The world is waiting to see the glory of God in the church—a reformation of His love, His righteousness, and His justice personally delivered to the poor and broken of all nations. But a spiritual reformation, as we will see, starts with a spiritual reformation of men.

Key Learnings

- A mountaintop event or experience for men is not sustainable if the local church does not have a partnership or back-end process to seize the moment and equip the men.
- Local church leadership can learn from these movements and become a willing partner rather than an obstacle for their men.
- Men need a place to express what they have just been exposed to and experienced in the parachurch event. This is your local church.

- It is imperative that the local church take ownership of the potentially catalytic outcomes of these events. Otherwise, we force men to wait 364 days for their next meaningful connection. Many won't make it.
- The local church mission, vision, initiatives, and values must be integral with the movement.
- Do not underestimate the power of a man's need for purpose, significance, legacy, and validation. If the church doesn't provide a context, someone will.
- Gatherings and events can be used to connect your men to a developmental process that will capture their imaginations.
- Men desire to use their gifts, passions, and abilities to serve the local church; embrace them with intention.
- Strong, moral, and spiritual pathways will guide men away from shallow cultural vision.

Chapter 5

No Move of God without Men of God, Part I

For if, by the trespass of the one man, death reigned through that one man, how much more will those who receive God's abundant provision of grace and of the gift of righteousness reign in life through the one man, Jesus Christ!

ROMANS 5:17

Ground zero.

The war in the garden, the fall, and the redemption of man can be captured in the character, conduct, and choices of two men. More poignantly, every man that has ever lived is "Act II" of this epic story: a generational, chromosomal, and spiritual microcosm spanning all ages, all cultures, and all peoples. All theology and history inexorably circles back around and lands in *this* context. Either men are in Adam or men are in Christ, creating blast zones of life or death in their windows of time and cultural contexts of existence. My opinion or feelings about this do not matter; neither does the debate over cosmology and biology as important as they are to origins. If one holds the Bible up as their source of authority (leaving God to sort out and manage the complexities), we are left with the biggest wheels of history turning on the small axles of two men and the spiritual realities they spawned. Depending on where you sit, this

> Depending on where you sit, this worldview can be labeled uneducated oversimplicity *or* essential biblical clarity.

worldview can be labeled uneducated over-simplicity *or* essential biblical clarity. I am choosing the latter. Death or life "reign" in the earth depending on the spiritual charac-ter and conduct of men.

Biblically, men are central *and* men are responsible.

The centrality of men as God's instru-ments of divine movement begets an equally powerful *responsibility* and *accountability* to God that should temper feelings of favorit-ism in the gender debates. His selection brings His *examination* and *investigation*. Notice: God calls Adam on the carpet to account for what befell the first couple in the garden and makes *him* explain himself first. He calls Eli to account for the actions of his sons, not the mother. He judges His leaders, His Kings, His priests, and His princes harshly for mishandling their mantles of influence over others. He sends special envoys to address or, in many cases, dress down His men because their character and conduct are out of whack. He charges fathers with material, relational, and spiritual responsibility for the marriage and family, placing a "lien" on the prayers of men who fail to respect the privilege of this ordained position. He refuses to listen to men who fail to lead women compassionately and justly (see Mal. 2:13–16; 1 Pet. 3:7). I could go on, but this must be placed in clear view as we begin what is, for many, a contentious claim.

The biblical fact of the primary role of men is terrifying to all who have suffered unjustly at the hands of men, and rightly so. There is no disputing the suffering and injustices throughout recorded history to now. This reality makes sympathy tough to come by for men, as the focus passes by them over to the victims of their beliefs and behaviors globally. The primary role of men and the close connection to injustice in recent decades has become the object of a social, political, and eco-nomic crusade for women and children worldwide, seeking to escape suffering, establish independence, and secure dignity. These movements are powerful, visible, and supported well by both genders, as well by high-profile media and entertainment figures who have been touched by the victims. In the media universe men are a caricature—allowed to be victimizers, comics, unreliable, adolescent, athletic, or Neanderthal for entertainment purposes only. In the sociopolitical nexus we are the makers of "glass ceilings," old-boy networks, and gender-suppressive infrastructures that need to be dismantled or overcome. In the digital age perception has become reality, and men are lost to themselves in, what feels to them, a losing battle for credibility. Struggling to respond the right way in the midst of the present masculine malaise is the church. An organization with a biblical mandate to equip and mobilize over half a billion affiliated men.

Overwhelming.

That is why, in the middle of cultural wars surrounding men, we need *biblical confidence,* which appears to be lacking. We need direct revelation from God on the subject of men and a strong faith response to what is discovered through an intentional search of the Scripture. Only when the fear of intentionally involving, investing in, and evangelistically pursuing men is replaced with a strong revelation of God's pattern and purpose for men will there be a realizing of the church's potential and promise. A new unity, identity, energy, and expression flowing from fresh revelation regarding his men will result in a powerful advance of God's purposes. The bride glows for her groom.

A move of God is experienced.

The inception of your church's men's movement must begin with a burning-bush encounter with God (not us) as it relates to men in your congregation and men in your community. Flowing from *that* encounter will come practical energy and a pursuit of God's will. That's the way you should want it, and that's the only way it will make sense for your local mission. We have taken hundreds of churches through the Sleeping Giant process spawning local and regional

> That is why, in the middle of cultural wars surrounding men, we need biblical confidence, which appears to be lacking.

men's movements around the world based on the following revelation and response progression.

Revelation and Response Process

Show Me Biblically (core revelation) → Prioritize Tactically (core recognition) → Move Intentionally (core reaction) → Without Apology (core reflection) → Growth Exponentially (core realization)

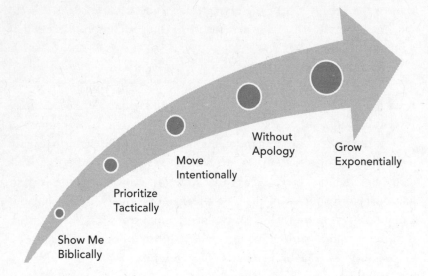

Show Me
Biblically

Prioritize
Tactically

Move
Intentionally

Without
Apology

Grow
Exponentially

After we have been shown *biblically,* then (and only then) can the church prioritize *tactically* and move *intentionally* without *apology.* The result? God's plans and purposes for your local body expands *exponentially* including growth in church health and numbers of families. This is always the math of great spiritual movement—a revelation and a faith response.

We see it. We want it. We pursue it.

First, you have to *see it.*

Exponential Movements of God	
Human Race	Adam
Covenant of Life	Noah
Covenant to Bless World	Abraham
Covenant of a Nation	Jacob and His Sons
Deliverance of Israel	Moses
Securing of Promised Land	Joshua
Judges to King	David
Prophetic Ministry	Isaiah to Malachi
Target of Prophetic Ministry	Men of Israel
Savior and Redeemer	Jesus Christ
Kingdom Announced	John the Baptist
Kingdom Advanced	12 Disciples
Birth of Church	Peter
Target Audience of Pentecost	"Men of Israel, listen"
Mission to Gentile World	Paul

This is an initial panorama of God's *major* moves, and they are undisputedly connected to selected men of *God's choosing.* All represent exponential turning points in God's plans on earth for certain ages and times. In each case men are selected, men are central to the movement, men are targeted, and men are held responsible. These movements through men are marked by significant bursts of God's spoken and active will as well as His energy spiritually, materially, physically, and emotionally. He blesses and disciplines. He delivers and destroys. He helps and allows to fail. He tests and tempts. He experiences elation with some. He endures frustration with others. *All those chosen are flawed* except the Son.

His moves. His choice. His way.

> His moves.
> His choice.
> His way.

It's one thing to see a simple pattern like this on the surface; it's another thing to study the pattern in depth. That's why we need to ask some or all of the following questions.

1. Why is each man important in the context of God's plan or pattern?
2. What problem or purpose are these leaders being called to address?
3. What are the obstacles to success?
4. How does God provide a solution? In what form?
5. What does it tell us about men in our congregations?
6. What is the lesson for pastors and leaders in the church today?

Some moves of God and the men connected to them highlight certain lessons better than others. Some provide a complete picture. All are consistent in the main applications when it comes to men. Each man of God has a life and leadership message God wants us to see. In this chapter we will take a close look at Adam, Abraham, Moses, and Joshua. In chapter 6 we are going to look at Jephthah, King David, King Josiah, and the prophets. And lastly, in chapter 7 we will look at Jesus, the disciples, Peter, the men of Pentecost, and the apostle Paul. Exploring the lives of these men is more than exploring biblical history and accumulating strategy. In fact, we hope that in the process you will come face-to-face with your own issues, specific problems in your congregation, and the explosive possibilities raised by a new revelation regarding men.

So let's begin at ground zero.

Thermonuclear Adam

> For if, by the trespass of the one man, death reigned through that one man, how much more will those who receive God's abundant provision of grace and of the gift of righteousness reign in life through the one man, Jesus Christ! (Rom. 5:17)

This is the *hindsight* of the apostle Paul reflecting on Adam, revisiting Jesus, and framing the gospel in the context of these two central figures. Hindsight is synonymous with greater clarity as you are now squarely on the other side of an experience or event looking back. Now, with 20/20 clarity, the expert in the law and survivor of a personal confrontation with the living Christ reflects and simplifies both the problem and the solution.

Key words: "one man."

One man brings death to many and puts people in a condition of separation from God. The other man brings life to many, redeeming their condition and connection. One man is the source of the problem. Another man is the solution. One is making the wrong choice in the garden of Eden, and the other is making the right choice in the garden of Gethsemane. One man cannot deny himself in the moment. The other denies himself comfort for a crucifixion. One says, "My will be done," and the other says, "Your will be done." One man triggers a cycle of suffering and tribulation. The other man triggers a cycle of salvation and transformation. One brings bondage to people, and the other brings freedom. The devil gets to apply the pressure to both. History and eternity hang in the balance.

Two men. Two choices. Two blast zones of impact.

What do you see when you see a man in your congregation or community? Scripture sees a stick of dynamite that is exploding its core character outward onto the people around them causing great collateral damage for good and God or for self and Satan. What do you see when you see a group of men in your congregation or community? Scripture sees thermonuclear potential with the capability of changing the fabric of communities and countries. Are men pivotal or incidental to the plan of God? Are the men in our radius of ministry under the same *targeted* moral and spiritual pressure? What are the consequences of the decisions men are making under that pressure for the local church, it's families, and the communities they find themselves in? Why all the questions you say? I'll say it until all pastors get it.

Your attitude about men reflects your ministry to men.

Biblically, men are like enriched uranium that can be weaponized and deployed into the spiritual battle. Their potential is powerful and, as such, they are central. If we see them this way, it means that we must take great care of the men in our possession and within our reach. It also means we *should be* making a concerted effort to prevent them from slipping into the hands of the terrorist and falling under his control. For every man we release to the influence of culture (believer and nonbeliever), we just need to remember that his core nature (in Adam) will explode death outward to those around him.

Adam was, and still is, ground zero.

Abraham's 318

When Abram heard that his relative had been taken captive, he called out the 318 trained men born in his own household and went in pursuit as far as Dan. During the night Abram divided his men to attack them and routed them, pursuing them as far as Hobah, north of Damascus. He recovered all the goods and brought back his relative Lot and his possessions, together with the women and other people. (Gen. 14:14–16)

Impressive.

Abraham's reaction to the news that four evil leaders had ransacked his nephew's city, looted its goods, and enslaved its citizens is, by all accounts, Spartanesque. The bad guys *had no idea* Lot had an uncle who could rain thunder and strike with lightning force with a mere "318." A nighttime raid. A precision attack. A dominating physical performance. Wow. All men who love their families, love justice, and love against-all-odds stories love this one. Go Abraham! But could it be that this account is here for more than a biblical high five?

More impressive is the untold but obvious story—*of leadership.*

> Biblically, men are like enriched uranium that can be weaponized and deployed into the spiritual battle.

- A leader with total command of *his* men.
- A leader who had intentionally invested in and trained men.

- A leader who is able to *"call out"* and his men suit up and show up.
- A leader who raised up men *"born in his own household."*
- A leader who knew how to skillfully deploy his men for victory.
- A leader capable of responding at a *moment's notice* with power and force.

The rest of the story does not disappoint either (Gen. 14:17–24). The leader and his men "recovered and brought back" the captives. The leader is blessed by Melchizidek, king of Salem and priest of the Most High God (the priestly order of Jesus himself). Abraham proceeds to unselfishly *accept nothing* for himself but turns over a handsome offer from a grateful king of Sodom to the *men who served him.* It is right after this demonstration of his leadership that God's man is rewarded, promised a son, and given a worldwide legacy (Gen. 15:1–6). This episode was *the tipping point* in Abraham's journey. Abram becomes Abraham. The key that unlocks the whole progression?

"He called out the 318 trained men born in his own household."

That is the "resonator" all pastors and shepherds should take away from Abraham as it relates to their own communities of men (or lack thereof). He had muscle for this mission, and that made him agile to the task. These men were a specially designated group of leaders known as "the 318." These *"were trained men,"* which means they had been taken through a *specific process* for a specific purpose—to serve Abraham's needs when called upon. These were also men he knew well, leaders raised up from his *"own household."* How many pastors have a designated community of men they can call on with such efficiency and economy? How many are thoughtfully bringing their men through an intentional process of leader development and deployment? How many have leadership engines like this coming out of their houses of worship?

> "He called out the 318 trained men born in his own household."

Ordinary Men Empowered by God

If Adam shows us the power, promise, and potential of men, then Abraham's thoughtful and intentional use of that energy sets the early template in Scripture for how to take advantage of it. That God thought highly of Abraham's faith is central to our understanding of him as a man; but, as we will see, God also thought highly of Abraham's "318" concept as we jump to the next move of God's being driven by men of God.

Gather. Give vision. Go!

Go, assemble the elders of Israel and say to them, "The Lord, the God of your fathers—the God of Abraham, Isaac and Jacob—appeared to me and said: I have watched over you and have seen what has been done to you in Egypt. And I have promised to bring you up out of your misery in Egypt into the land of the Canaanites, Hittites, Amorites, Perizzites, Hivites and Jebusites—a land flowing with milk and honey." The elders of Israel will listen to you. Then you and the elders are to go to the king of Egypt and say to him, "The Lord, the God of the Hebrews, has met with us. Let us take a three-day journey into the wilderness to offer sacrifices to the Lord our God." But I know that the king of Egypt will not let you go unless a mighty hand compels him. So I will stretch out my hand and strike the Egyptians with all the wonders that I will perform among them. After that, he will let you go. (Exod. 3:16–20)

What do we see?

We see God. We see Moses. We see the mission that Moses is called by God to execute. We see Moses being pointed intentionally by God Himself to an infrastructure of leaders He has placed around him. But what does God tell him to do with this group of men? What's the process?

1. Gather them ("*assemble the elders*")

2. Give the vision (*"say to [them], 'the LORD the God of your fathers'"* etc.)
3. God gives Moses' men insight into the vision (*"the elders will listen to you"*)
4. Go speak to the most powerful man in the known world together!
5. Get ready for a show of my power.

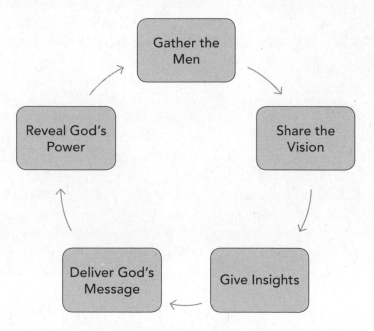

We have already gotten a snapshot of Moses in ministry needing a strong infrastructure of men to shepherd the people in chapter 2. In this flashback Moses is sent on his first combat mission flying straight into the belly of the beast to knock heads with the most powerful man in the known world. The mission: Take his labor force! It's an overwhelming task, but God has planned exact support to meet the needs of his leader physically, emotionally, spiritually, and relationally for the mother of all road trips any group of men has ever taken. Bottom line: he would not be alone in the mission.

His men would be behind him all the way.

> I want my pastor to have plenty of leaders who will be able to walk with him into the missions and visions God has called him to execute locally and globally.

This is the exact sentiment that fuels me as pastor of men at Saddleback. I want my pastor to have plenty of leaders who will be able to walk with him into the missions and visions God has called him to execute locally and globally. I see the pattern of Scripture and so does he. I want my pastor to know that he is not alone and there are leaders at his disposal to share the load in every way. In fact, he meets with the men's leadership just as Moses met with his leaders *prior to major campaigns and initiatives*. All he has to do is call me. When we meet, he shares the vision God has planted in him and seeks to execute through him *along with us*. Then he tells us what he needs. We pray for our pastor and then we "go" on mission. We will talk about building a leader engine in Section III, but for now we want you to see plainly God's intentional work with Moses in ministry and on mission. *God says:* Gather the men, give them the vision I gave you, I will give insight to them, and then call them to go with you into the battle!

While Moses would cycle in and out of an awareness of his need for a strong network of men behind him and experience massive deficits of physical and emotional energy, his apprentice was paying attention and taking notes. By all indicators Joshua was an emotional wreck upon the death of Moses, the transfer of the mantle of leadership, and on the eve of moving a million plus people into occupied foreign lands. You don't tell a man who's feeling strong and courageous already to be "strong and courageous." You give that encouragement to a man who feels weak, afraid, and inadequate to the task at hand. Joshua chapter 1 has welcomed many a frightened leader in God's army! We have spent many hours in this powerful chapter of Scripture, battling the same emotions Joshua did and receiving God's words to Joshua afresh for ourselves as we summon the faith and courage to show up to assignments much bigger than ourselves. And while he may have needed some encouragement and inspiration, Moses' replacement was a master at mobilizing of the people.

The Network

"Have I not commanded you? Be strong and courageous. Do not be afraid; do not be discouraged, for the LORD your God will be with you wherever you go." So Joshua ordered the officers of the people: "Go through the camp and tell the people, 'Get your provisions ready. Three days from now you will cross the Jordan here to go in and take possession of the land the LORD your God is giving you for your own.'" (Josh. 1:9–11)

Connectivity.

It is a precious commodity in the leadership world. With it you can move your organization through changes and challenges much easier and with greater facility than those who lack it. Those leaders who lack connectivity among their people move slowly and painfully without a system of reliable relationships to mobilize the larger community. And while a lot of leaders claim to have a great team and structure in their organizations, they really don't know the strength of the their "network" until it's tested and the depth of its traction produces real movement forward.

Key word: *traction.*

After God stabilizes Joshua's emotional and spiritual spine, the only reason he is able take action is because his organization has *serious traction.* Top to bottom, his network runs deeply and relationally from his inner core all the way to the outer communities of his people. We need to highlight two features of his network. First, his network is made up of men. Second, they are assigned specific groupings that they are responsible for messaging and mobilizing. They are called *officers of the people.*

> Top to bottom, his network runs deeply and relationally from his inner core all the way to the outer communities of his people.

Without the officers of the people there is no ability to form ranks around a single direction or vision whether you are moving people across a river like Joshua or moving people through a giving and building campaign like David. When it is real, relationally solid, and received well by the people, *nothing can touch it.* What Joshua possessed thousands of years ago would still outperform the best digital networks available to us today in terms of people "buying in" with their heart *and* with their feet. A good network of connected leaders emanating from the leader outward saves money, saves time, and saves you from the negative emotions and pressures associated with trying to move a stubborn donkey forward. (I mean your congregation!) At least that's how *you perceive* the situation. You have awesome weekend attendance but awful initiative performance, and it's confusing, depressing, and infuriating—especially when the cause is Christ!

> What Joshua possessed thousands of years ago would still outperform the best digital networks available to us today.

Sound familiar?

Traction is possible but only when, like Joshua, you intentionally layer into your structure:

1. Men who report to you on a personal level (*Joshua ordered the officers*)
2. Men who reach into the network you lead (*go throughout the camp*)
3. Men who will repeat your words (*tell the people*)
4. Men who get respect when they direct others (*get ready*)
5. Men who relay your measure of faith (*you will go in and take possession*)

That first circle of leadership led to second and third circles that had to perform as well as the first circle in order to gain quality traction and movement across the network.

It was a must then. It is a must today.

My prayer is that you are detecting God's pattern and sensing His revelation through the Scripture for the Sleeping Giant in your congregation and community. The good news is that there are plenty of great men to draw from in your congregation and in your community to build an effective and explosive men's leadership engine. As you have been called to reach men through your church, the Holy Spirit is calling the men you will catch in your nets. Pray for them right now if you feel led. Pray for men you know. Pray for the men God brings to mind. Pray for the men yet unsaved and unconnected in your community. After that, pray for yourself, that God will seal your call to reach men and continue to open your eyes to His plans for you to reach them personally, locally in your church, and globally.

Buckle up.

Key Learnings

- All movements of God in men can be traced back to a defining moment in the choices of two men—Adam and Jesus. Two blast zones. Two different results.
- The character and conduct of men have a profound influence on the destiny of life and death on earth.
- People have suffered unjustly as a result of the men's irresponsibility with what God has given them.
- A strong revelation of God's pattern of the purpose for men can have strong implications for the local church if embraced and intentionally cultivated.
- Show men biblically, prioritize tactically, move intentionally without apology, and the men of your church can be activated exponentially to His work.
- Each man of God has a life and leadership calling on his life that God wants him to see.
- The church must intentionally provide an environment to develop what God has already placed in every man.

- Called leaders will serve others unselfishly and take nothing out of selfish motivation.
- Can your church say it has a vibrant and robust leadership development pipeline?
- Kingdom assignments are bigger than each of our men. They will need the support of the church and one another.

Chapter 6

No Move of God
without Men of God,
Part II

*Jephthah said to them, "Didn't you hate me and drive
me from my father's house? Why do you come to me now,
when you're in trouble?" The elders of Gilead said to
him, "Nevertheless, we are turning to you now."*

Judges 11:7–8

Stupid mistakes.

Mine are legend. I thank God that He doesn't say to me, "Well, you got yourself into this mess, and you can get yourself out of it!" Instead He provides the mercy that allows me to escape the harsh consequences of my blunders. Like the *one time* I forgot my wedding anniversary and didn't realize until the morning of. I looked at my watch and there was "6–18" (June 18) staring back at me, a small pause and then . . . "Aaaaah!" I slipped out of the house and hurried to the grocery store to get a plant, some coffee, and a fifty-cent card. I returned feeling like the bacteria that live on the scum that sits at the bottom of the trash can in the men's subway restroom. I was lower than low in the face of a reality that none of my usual resourcefulness or smooth talking could erase or make better. Staring at my wife's face as I handed her the plant was a snapshot that is burned forever on my brain. I was praying she wouldn't ask the ten-million-pound question: "You forgot, didn't you?" She did. The plant begged the question because *normally* I plot and plan for days over what I am going to do for anniversaries and then do the "big reveal" sometime that day. So with my tail between my legs and no excuses, leverage, assets, bargaining power, or rationale to give *other than* I had made a mistake—I owned up. Ever been there?

Awkward.

As we journey forward out of the patriarchs in the Old Testament and over to the time of judges, kings, and prophets, there are both awesome and awkward moments to explore. But the template and pattern of God among His men is consistent and constant as ever. The promise and potential of men remain, but not all leaders realize how valuable having a strong infrastructure of men is, especially during times of peace and comfort. But as challenges arise, as leadership needs grow, as the spiritual health of God's people is jeopardized by the surrounding culture, and as God's character is put to the test, we see the familiar intervention—the men. So let's take a look at some select snapshots from the ages of the judges, kings, and prophets and reaffirm the scriptural foundations of the Sleeping Giant revelation and response process. Far from being limited in time and place, all of the examples we explore have a targeted message for pastors and churches today. Especially, the story and lessons God provides us in Scripture out of the life and leadership journey of our first leader from the age of judges.

This might sting a little.

You Decide: A Man of Peace or a Man of War?

Jephthah the Gileadite was a mighty warrior. His father was Gilead; his mother was a prostitute. Gilead's wife also bore him sons, and when they were grown up, they drove Jephthah away. "You are not going to get any inheritance in our family," they said, "because you are the son of another woman." So Jephthah fled from his brothers and settled in the land of Tob, where a gang of scoundrels gathered around him and followed him.

Some time later, when the Ammonites were fighting against Israel, the elders of Gilead went to get Jephthah from the land of Tob. "Come," they said, "be our commander, so we can fight the Ammonites." Jephthah said to them, "Didn't you hate me and drive me from my father's house? Why do you come to me now, when you're in trouble?" The elders of Gilead said to him, "Nevertheless, we are turning to you now; come with us to fight the Ammonites, and you will be head over all of us who live in Gilead." (Judg. 11:1–8)

Awkward.

Flash way back: Jephthah's dad sleeps with a prostitute, and he is the product of the infidelity. He is labeled as illegitimate his whole life, and his family is pressured by the religious establishment to minimize this dark blot on their religious culture. (Notice he doesn't blame his family, but the "elders of Gilead.") For the elders his presence has become too emotionally heavy to bear, and the family is complicit for its own reasons. It takes a while, but eventually his half brothers leverage Jephthah's baggage against him divesting him fully *out of the only community of faith, family, and future he knows.*

Orphaned by your own.

That "orphan spirit," and its boiling need for validation, finds a new family and expression in foreign lands. More specifically, he *"settled in the land of Tob, where a group of scoundrels gathered around him and followed him."* Jephthah becomes somebody—a strong and infamous "somebody" who commands men and handles a sword with deadly efficiency. This particular "embarrassment" becomes a celebrity with serious swagger, and this plot just keeps getting thicker. In fact, it's so thick you can slice the humiliation with a knife as the elders of Gilead are forced to ask their "unfavorite" son to defend the people who left him out in the cold. During the peaceful years peaceful men worked just fine. They didn't add or take away any value, and there was no need to train them for war. Israel got lazy and indifferent during times of peace (and usually ended up sinning more). But now, with Ammonite thunder about to reign down on Israel, those kind of men just won't do.

The solution? *The land of Tob.*

In the land of Tob, you find men that religious culture looks down on as unredeemable or untouchable. They are a little rougher around the edges and didn't go to Christian prep school. They have been through a lot, suffered a lot, and had to become resourceful at a young age *not by choice.* They are a mix of anger, fear, ambition, anxiety, and self-loathing. Like all men who have been orphaned, they are on a quest for sonship and validation, which causes them to prostitute themselves to any identity or connection that feeds their deep need for significance and belonging. In the end the power of rejection has been repurposed and reinvigorated toward the one thing all orphan spirits crave—to feel worthy whatever it takes.

> Like all men who have been orphaned, they are on a quest for sonship and validation, which causes them to prostitute themselves to any identity.

The orphan mighty warrior.

Jephthah is the type of man the church needs desperately today to bring needed strength, skill, ability, and courage. Millions of men inside and outside the church searching for transcendence, strong meaning, a strong cause, and strong connections with other men who help deliver God's justice. They have been driven from the Father's house, orphaned, and forced to find their worth somewhere else, helping someone else, and *serving* someone else.

Not only does this reality sting, but the price is steep. The peaceful men (the affiliated) filling our churches cannot meet the demands of an active assault against the mission, people, and purposes of God.

> The peaceful men (the affiliated) filling our churches cannot meet the demands of an active assault against the mission, people, and purposes of God.

The risk takers are somewhere else doing something daring and adventuresome. With those assets gone, pastors have no "land of Tob" to call on for muscle, energy, strength, spiritual courage, and a willingness to sacrifice for the things God declares to be significant. *"From the days of John the Baptist until now, the kingdom of heaven has been forcefully advancing, and forceful men lay hold of it" (Matt. 11:12).* Did you hear him?

Forceful kingdom movements require forceful men.

As you follow God's people, when Israel was not at war, it fell into complacency, idolatry, and sin. When they were at war, they were focused and faithful, *advancing and possessing* the next place of God's purpose. The persecuted church moves and feels the same way. But now God's Spirit is rising in His church worldwide and calling it forward for a forceful advance and spiritual harvest. To do that God wants His men back serving with Him (versus the world) and gobbling up lots of spiritual real estate for the kingdom. Like the elders of Gilead, we need to "go get Jephthah from the land of Tob," proactively pursuing men we have dismissed to other realms of existence. We also need to humbly borrow a line from them.

> Forceful kingdom movements require forceful men.

"Nevertheless, we are turning to you now."

Key word: *nevertheless.* Need-based reconciliation like that of the elders of Gilead and Jephthah requires humility and faith from both parties because of the *history.* I have spoken to many pastors who have such a bad taste in their mouth about men's ministry because the men behind the ministry went "rogue" and served their vision versus the vision of the church. Likewise, millions of men in the church are wondering if they are even needed because they have never been personally acknowledged as valuable to the enterprise and invited into the vision by their pastors. Right now God is calling pastors and their men to set aside the disconnecting issue or past reality in order to take hold of the kingdom reality to which we all belong.

Watch the film as the elders of Gilead and Jephthah have their moment.

> Jephthah answered, "Suppose you take me back to fight the Ammonites and the LORD gives them to me—will I really be your head?" The elders of Gilead replied, "The LORD is our witness; we will certainly do as you say." So Jephthah went with the elders of Gilead, and the people made him head and commander over them. And he repeated all his words before the LORD in Mizpah. (Judg. 11:9–11)

> Like the elders of Gilead, we need to "go get Jephthah from the land of Tob."

The result of this reconciliation and reaffirmation of his value is that Israel gets twenty straight victories and subdues Ammon. The parable for the church is both unmistakable and widely available if it chooses to aggressively advance the kingdom and aggressively invest in finding the right men for the job. The revelation? Strong advances require strong men. If you have them, engage them intentionally now. If you don't, go and get them back. Your capacity to extend your reach and your ability to survive the assaults that are coming depend on it. Jephthah is the man we need for this hour.

King David shows how to use him.

David's First Move

David summoned all the officials of Israel to assemble at Jerusalem: the officers over the tribes, the commanders of the divisions in the service of the king, the commanders of thousands and commanders of hundreds, and the officials in charge of all the property and livestock belonging to the king and his sons, together with the palace officials, the mighty men and all the brave warriors. King David rose to his feet and said: "Listen to me, my brothers and my people. I had it in my heart to build a house as a place of rest for the ark of the covenant of the LORD, for the footstool of our God, and I made plans to build it." (1 Chron. 28:1–2)

Big visions are just big words *without* big muscle behind the big mouth.

Big Mission + Big Muscle = Big Movement

David's "land of Tob" was in his hip pocket. He is the envy of all pastors who have trouble rallying their congregations to the vision of the church. David has no hurdles to overcome or "rogue" men he has to reign in. He didn't need to pander to special interests or big check writers. He didn't need to print materials or hold special dinners to warm up the faithful givers. All of his men were present, and all were on board. He had traction.

Here is where we see the pattern: *God, a man, a vision, and a network of men supporting the leader top to bottom.* The steps are simple, but we can't forget that David's own integrity, his own example, own training in command structure, and own commitment to surrounding himself with strong leaders (read Ps. 101) worked as the operational foundation. And God put it here in the Bible for every pastor to see, marvel at, imitate, and strive to implement so that he, too, can fulfill the vision God has flooded his Spirit with as well.

How does the man after God's heart follow a vision God gave him?

1. Summon the men. David has nine layers of men that represent the height,

> The picture of leader support should be the goal of any men's pastor or men's ministry leader.

depth, width, and reach of his men's network. These men are clearly the primary stakeholders and the secret to his present and ongoing success. He honors them by calling them together first before presenting the vision to the larger faith community. The leaders listed first are the "officers of the tribes" who are connected to the people. *Then* comes his own palace people who serve and protect them. Within the circle of male leadership, those who are actually touching the people are primary, *not* the other way around.

David's ability to summon the men like this is a worthy and *doable* goal. We like to plant this vision *in your mind* so that we can begin with the end in mind and load the process to achieve it within your particular church structure. This picture of leader support should be the goal of any men's pastor or men's ministry leader: *to give your pastor a network that is free, personal, relationally connected, and fast acting.*

2. Share the vision with the men. With the men as first hearers, you tell the story of what God has been telling you, how He told you, what exactly you are going to do, and what the spiritual purpose is behind it. Men serving in a local church feel so honored to be the first ones to hear, possess, own this tribal knowledge, and then be commissioned to deliver information they alone know to their families. It places them in relationship with the leader, vests them as carriers of the vision, and establishes them as ambassadors of the vision. David, and any pastor for that matter, who has a structure of men's ministry that can do this helps himself while he strengthens the bonds he has with his men.

> Pastors should be raising up wise, spiritually related sons to lead the change for the visions God has in their hearts.

3. Strengthen the men. In a brilliant stroke David models for all pastors and leaders of men the highest priority of the whole process: spiritual integrity. His bigger concern was to make sure his men and his managers were undivided in their hearts and that they were doing it together. Once the vision was received, affirmed, and cast, David focused solely on leading his men spiritually through the process of seeing the vision to completion. He was shepherding his men as all good pastors should. He didn't dance. He charged his men to closely guard their spiritual integrity. The message: their beliefs and behaviors mattered more than buildings.

4. Select the leader. *"Of all my sons—and the Lord has given me many—he has chosen my son Solomon to sit on the throne of the kingdom of the Lord over Israel. He said to me: 'Solomon your son is the one who will build my house and my courts, for I have chosen him to be my son, and I will be his father'"* (1 Chron. 28:5–6). David has a wise, blood-related son who is gifted and chosen to lead the men in the undertaking. He will be hands-on and coordinating the troops. He will execute the vision along with the other skilled men. He will have proximity to the leader's thoughts and plans. Likewise, pastors should be raising up wise, spiritually related sons to lead the charge for the visions God has in their hearts. Versus what? Versus hiring so many leaders from the outside. Your leaders should be close to you, think like you, be loyal to you, and be from your own household. To be able to say publicly, "This is my guy," publicly brings with it a lot of credibility.

> Encouragement is the oxygen of leader development and requires relationship.

5. Strengthen the leader. *"And you, my son Solomon, acknowledge the God of your father, and serve him with wholehearted devotion and with a willing mind, for the Lord searches every heart and understands every desire and every thought. If you seek him, he will be found by you; but if you forsake him, he will reject you forever. Consider now, for the Lord has chosen you to build a house as a sanctuary. Be strong and do the work"* (1 Chron. 28:9–10). Encouragement is the oxygen of leader development and requires relationship. David starts by reminding his son that the inner life is first and dwells there. Motives, devotion, and inward agreement with God are the bedrock, not the actual bedrock. From that place of inner strength and integrity at the top, he can launch into the work.

6. Support the leader with other leaders. *"David also said to Solomon his son, 'Be strong and courageous, and do the work. Do not be* *afraid or discouraged, for the Lord God, my God, is with you. He will not fail you or forsake you until all the work for the service of the temple of the Lord is finished. The divisions of the priests and Levites are ready for all the work on the temple of God, and every willing person skilled in any craft will help you in all the work. The officials and all the people will obey your every command'"* (1 Chron. 28:20–21). PHEW! Can you imagine Solomon's look of relief after David tells him that it's not all on him. First, that God will be working onsite and alongside him. Good to know! Second, dedicated groups of God's men will be assisting. Third, skilled specialists will work in even the smallest spaces of the project. Fourth, they will be great to work with. Show your leaders how the network works!

1. God
2. A man
3. A vision
4. A network of leaders to support that vision

God's pattern and purpose for men in the church is to be leading and supporting the vision of the leader God has selected, to be under spiritual authority, and to serve the Lord with their specific skill sets until the vision is complete. God models this through the man after His heart so that other men after His heart in future generations can see their visions achieved or God glorified.

The result: Big visions are more than big words because the church has big muscle.

Josiah's on Fire!

Then the king called together all the elders of Judah and Jerusalem. He went up to the temple of the LORD with the men of Judah, the people of Jerusalem, the priests and the prophets—all the people from the least to the greatest. He read in their hearing all the words of the Book of the Covenant, which had been found in the temple of the LORD. The king stood by the pillar and renewed the covenant in the presence of the LORD—to follow the LORD and keep his commands, regulations and decrees with all his heart and all his soul, thus confirming the words of the covenant written in this book. Then all the people pledged themselves to the covenant. The king ordered Hilkiah the high priest, the priests next in rank and the doorkeepers to remove from the temple of the LORD all the articles made for Baal and Asherah and all the starry hosts. He burned them outside Jerusalem in the fields of the Kidron Valley and took the ashes to Bethel. (2 Kings 23:1–4)

"You can't do that!"

Ever heard those words? I am sure Josiah did when the whole topic of idols in the land came up. What made him think he could rid the land of idols when so many kings, even good ones like Hezekiah and Asa could not do it. But in the tradition and spirit of David, Josiah decides the Word comes first over the world and that his leaders will be the ones to heed the words of God and honor the heart of God. He resolves that idolatry will end under his watch and that this spiritual disease infecting his lands, polluting their worship, and introducing sin will be no more. His steps are noticeably familiar and worth noting because this is a major move of God among His people to create spiritual health in the community of faith.

1. He called together the leaders (elders of Jerusalem).
2. He called the men of Judah to lead their families.
3. He called the people to follow.
4. He read all the words of the Book of the Covenant.

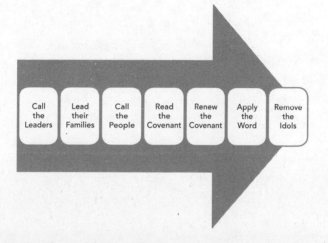

5. He renewed the covenant in God's presence.

6. He applied the Word.

7. He commissioned His men to remove the idols—no exceptions.

A one-of-a-kind king with one-of-a-kind men serving their leader in a one-of-a-kind movement never to be repeated.

> Neither before nor after Josiah was there a king like him who turned to the LORD as he did—with all his heart and with all his soul and with all his strength, in accordance with all the Law of Moses. (2 Kings 23:25)

Josiah had a Sleeping Giant just waiting to go to work for him, but he did a couple of things that activated them to do things never before done.

1. He honored the Word of God aggressively.

2. He delivered the Word of God aggressively to his men.

3. He emphasized applying the Word of God aggressively and "fulfilling the requirements of the law."

4. He repented and "turned to the Lord" publicly.

The lesson: Strong personal actions *for God* rally strong men to God.

Both David and Josiah led major moves of God in the land and built their efforts from their own hearts outward to the hearts of the men. When the kings led the men well, the people responded well to their kings. Both clearly put time and energy into the relationships they had with their leaders because their leaders delivered. And while many other kings connected to God in unique ways and had unique stories, these two are special in that they led their men intentionally and experienced major spiritual shifts or moved major initiatives forward.

> The lesson: Strong personal actions *for God* rally strong men to God.

They are showing us how to wake our own Sleeping Giant.

Key Learnings

- God's plan for developing men has been constant and consistent.
- Ignored men that are not activated by the church will find significance in what culture has to offer, finding their worth outside the church context.
- The peacemakers will replace the risk-takers in your church and inhibit much-needed strength, skill, abilities, and courage to reach the masses.
- Living examples of great integrity, training, and commitment provide an operational foundation for your men's ministry. These men are primary to the goal.
- Frequent communication of the bigger vision honors those who are first to hear and have a chance to embrace and own the vision.
- Inward agreement with God is the bedrock of strong leaders. Leaders will exhibit the heart of God. God will equip the called, not necessarily call the equipped.

Chapter 7

Eyeing the Men

*The vineyard of the LORD Almighty is the house of
Israel, and the men of Judah are the garden of his
delight. And he looked for justice, but saw bloodshed;
for righteousness, but heard cries of distress.*

ISAIAH 5:7

Problems seldom live at the level at which they are seen.

As a counselor for a mental health company, I learned quickly how
to get to the bottom of what was happening in the lives of people. It was
a systematic approach that peeled away people's defense mechanisms,
eliminated their excuses, broke through their blaming, forced them to
face their fears and recognize reality. I would start with benign questions
like: "Where are you from?" and, "How did you find out about our program?" After building a little rapport, learning their name, and getting
some basic contact information, I would dive in and ask: "So how can I
help you today?" This question was the first "tell" or signal of how the
conversation was going to go and how long I would be on the phone. I
would know within the first sixty seconds of a person's response to that
question whether or not they were ready to get help.

Time for small talk was over.

Like a surgeon being handed a scalpel, I would break the skin, ask for retractors, open these folks up, and start hunting for the real problem or issue. I *already knew* there was a serious problem on the other end of the line because people, especially men, prefer to resolve issues privately, and they only call a stranger when it's really bad. I became good at raising the "mirror of reality," and if the pain of their situation exceeded their fear of changing, we could make some great progress. Between the pain and the fear was *me*. So to help people get there, I would say, "Well, what we have here is not a little scrape, or a cut, or even a deep cut. This one is a big bleeder. You see that, right?" A no would be like trying to deny being shot in the chest. "A little Band-Aide solution is not going to help you much with a big bleeder, right? Big bleeders require major surgery. Or else what continues to happen?" Then, after a pause, the answer would come. *"It just keeps bleeding."*

The problem was obvious. Gaining agreement required work.

All of the prophets in the Bible (major and minor) are commissioned by God to expose the "big bleeder" with God's people: *a broken covenant.* The problems manifesting themselves among the people had a deeper root cause, and a prophet was called on to expose both the symptoms and the source.

> The problem was obvious. Gaining agreement required work.

Sometimes God would send a prophet to warn Israel of impending judgment related to a break. Other prophets were sent to encourage God's people in the midst of judgment and captivity that God would restore the nation. Then there were the "clean up" prophets, the ones who came on the scene *after* God's people were released from judgment and captivity. These men were sent to assure Israel that God would relate in a covenant way once again and remind them that He was sovereign in His use of other nations to discipline them. The final tally?

- Over three hundred years of prophetic ministry
- Sixteen different messengers
- Four different geographic regions

- Total agreement on the source behind the big break with covenant—God's men.

The historical foundation and backdrop was Moab. There, God
through His leader Moses assigns responsibility for the health of Israel's
relationship with God to the men of Israel. Clear terms, projected blessings and curses, and a strong exhortation impressed upon a particular
segment of the audience.

> Carefully follow the terms of this covenant, so that you may
> prosper in everything you do. All of you are standing today in
> the presence of the LORD your God—your leaders and chief
> men, your elders and officials, and all the other men of Israel,
> together with your children and your wives, and the aliens liv-
> ing in your camps who chop your wood and carry your water.
> (Deut. 29:10–11)

That men will carry the mantle of this charge to *"carefully follow
the terms of this covenant"* is implicit on many levels. The first level is
categorically: three distinct groups are present, separated, categorized,
and assigned a standing in the midst of the "charge" by Moses.

Group 1	Group 2	Group 3
Leaders	Wives	Aliens
Chief Men	Children	
Elders		
Officials		
All Other Men of Israel		

"All" are present, but only one group is central and responsible in
God's eyes—Group 1. Those *together with* or tethered to the primary
receivers of Moses' charge by family or employment ties are those who
are covered by the mantle of the men. When it comes to keeping a covenant people healthy, Group 1 is like the lead engine pulling the other
train cars (Groups 2 and 3) behind it. If the lead engine decides to stay

on track, switch tracks, or falls off the tracks, *everyone else connected is right behind them in that path.* A lot is riding on the heart direction of Group 1.

The second level is sociological: the gender roles and responsibilities have the laser sited squarely on the chests of the men. The third level is historical: the recorded testimony of the prophets themselves assign the breaking of the covenant to the men directly and indirectly. The fourth level is theological: God says it specifically as we will see shortly. The fifth level is grammatical: terms, words, pictures, and metaphors are used by prophets which directly connect men and male behavior to the problem; the expressions simply cannot apply to the opposite sex. The sixth level is anthropological: the symptom behaviors or "backslidings" linked to the spiritual drift are male-centric.

> Men's health and the spiritual health of God's people are synonymous.

Men's health and the spiritual health of God's people are synonymous.

If the men heed Moses' warning and follow wholeheartedly, the connected blast radius is littered with blessing and life for those connected. If they fail, that same blast zone is characterized by certain judgment and destruction for all three groups. Because of that fact, Moses wants to burn one thought on the brains of all the men present: "I am responsible now." Imagine the following words hitting your ears as your wife and children stand next to you.

See, I set before you today life and prosperity, death and destruction. For I command you today to love the LORD your God, to walk in his ways, and to keep his commands, decrees and laws; then you will live and increase, and the LORD your God will bless you in the land you are entering to possess. But if your heart turns away and you are not obedient, and if you are drawn away to bow down to other gods and worship them, I declare to you this day that you will certainly be destroyed. You will not live long in the land you are crossing the Jordan to enter and possess. (Deut. 30:15–18)

It's God or other gods. It's covenant or culture.

If sons of covenant abandon their identity and become sons of culture *on the inside,* it spells trouble for *everyone.* With this context as the backdrop of all prophetic ministry and messages, a new and powerful lens of meaning infuses the words of these bold messengers. It also assigns fresh meaning to "new covenant" men, our battle to stay faithful sons of Christ, and evil attempts to draw us over to become sons of culture. Listen to Jesus strike this prophetic tone in His final moments with His disciples, *"If you belonged to the world ["kosmos" in Greek or cultural system of belief], it would love you as its own. As it is, you do not belong to the world [kosmos], but I have chosen you out of the world [kosmos]. That is why the world [kosmos] hates you" (John 15:19, brackets are mine).* The battle *then* (in the time of the prophets) was the battle *to come* (time of Jesus) and is the battle *now* for every man. All prophets were frontline warriors in this war for the covenant identity, energy, and expression of God's men. Their message?

> If sons of covenant abandon their identity and become sons of culture *on the inside,* it spells trouble for *everyone.*

Time for small talk is over.

One Sad Dad

I will sing for the one I love a song about his vineyard. My loved one had a vineyard on a fertile hillside. He dug it up and cleared it of stones and planted it with the choicest vines. He built a watchtower in it and cut out a winepress as well. Then he looked for a crop of good grapes, but it yielded only bad fruit. "Now you dwellers in Jerusalem and men of Judah, judge between me and my vineyard. What more could have been done for my vineyard than I have done for it? When I looked for good grapes, why did it yield only bad? Now I will tell you

what I am going to do to my vineyard: I will take away its
hedge, and it will be destroyed; I will break down its wall, and it
will be trampled. I will make it a wasteland, neither pruned nor
cultivated, and briers and thorns will grow there. I will command the clouds not to rain on it." The vineyard of the LORD
Almighty is the house of Israel, and the men of Judah are the
garden of his delight. And he looked for justice, but saw bloodshed; for righteousness, but heard cries of distress. (Isa. 5:1–7)

God provides a place of promise, abundant provision, and strong
protection in the land. He plants a "vineyard" (His people) in the land
to take advantage of this amazing destination after their deliverance.
He looks for "fruit" or "good grapes" (positive spiritual and character
growth) to flow out of such a fertile context, but to His deep disappointment He finds only "bad fruit." The obvious questions are:

1. So where's the bad apple that spoiled the whole bunch in God's
   eyes?
2. What "fruit" was He looking for exactly?
3. Who was He tracking in the process?
4. What does that reveal about His purpose and pattern with His
   people?
5. What was the impact on the community of faith?
6. What are the implications for the church, its leaders, and its men?

Look no further than "Group 1" for the answers to all these questions. God declares there is "everyone" *(the vineyard of the Lord Almighty
is the house of Israel)* and then there is Group 1 *(and the men of Judah are
the garden of his delight).* The picture is that of the owner of the vineyard
coming to inspect. The "garden" was where kings would showcase their
majesty and greatness through displaying their prized and exotic plants,
flowers, and greenery that came back to them from all over the known
world. They were a reflection of his power and had an encouraging effect
on kings who possessed them. The famous hanging gardens of Babylon,
which came into existence during the reigns of Nebuchadnezzar and
Sennacherib, provide a historical backdrop to the use of this metaphor.

The "garden of his delight" represents a place where God Himself goes to be ministered to, a place that gives Him joy, a place of pride, a place He takes a keen personal interest in, and it is a place that is set apart from the whole. It is special.

Turning points with God's plan revolve around the garden.

Adam had his. Jesus had His. And the men of Judah (God's men) have theirs. The decisions made in those gardens have big implications for a lot of people, and this is no different. The men of Judah that God planted in this special place to grow, to thrive, and to know Him have crossed the line and broken themselves away from their covenant identity and responsibility. He comes to the garden looking for "righteousness" and "justice" and, instead, is confronted with "bloodshed" and "cries of distress." As a men's pastor this whole scene puts what I do in a whole new light. And for every pastor worldwide this window into the heart of God for men should do the same. Simple application would be to ask ourselves:

1. What does God see when He looks upon "the garden of his delight" (the men) in my church?
2. How are the men of my congregation impacting those in their immediate blast zones of influence?
3. Does He see the "good fruit" of Christlikeness coming out of our body of men?
4. Does He see compassionate and strong justice flowing from the actions of our men?
5. Or does He see suffering and hear cries of distress from the people connected to their character and conduct?
6. What are the consequences for God's people when the health of God's men is not there?

Let's allow God Himself to answer that last question for us from His own Word and translate the profound spiritual import of what that means for the church.

Therefore, my people will go into exile for lack of understanding; their men of rank will die of hunger and their masses will be parched with thirst. . . . Therefore, as tongues of fire lick up straw and as the dry grass sinks down in the flames, so their roots will decay and their flowers will blow away like dust; for they have rejected the law of the LORD Almighty and spurned the word of the Holy One of Israel. (Isa. 5:13, 24)

Men acting *culturally* while living in the middle of *covenant community*. God's feeling about this makes me tremble as a man and shudder as a pastor. It is no secret that (both empirically and subjectively) this is the reality in the church today. And while I do not see foreign nations being sent to discipline the church as a whole, I do see *our men* living in exile spiritually and personally. I see the masses suffering. I see the foundations of churches rocked to the core. I see captivity everywhere with bondages of the flesh and strongholds of the mind oppressing our men, especially among spiritual leaders. I see the roots of the church decaying without the rooting of our men. I see the beauty of our local bodies unable to fully blossom in the absence of the brightness and strength men add to the body of Christ. God's strong response also provides powerful motivation for the church worldwide to begin engaging the Sleeping Giant revelation and response process. God's Word in the prophetic period of ministry *is prophetic for us!* It shows us just how personally God tracks, monitors, cares about, and is invested in the hearts of His men in the community of faith.

> Men's health and the spiritual health of God's people are synonymous.

So if that really is His *consistent* heart for His men, then what's ours?

Let the following prophetic messages and moments further reveal God's heart as He calls out to sons of covenant in jeopardy of becoming sons of culture.

"Circumcise" Your Hearts

"If you will return, O Israel, return to me," declares the LORD. "If you put your detestable idols out of my sight and

no longer go astray, and if in a truthful, just and righteous way
you swear, 'As surely as the LORD lives,' then the nations will
be blessed by him and in him they will glory. **This is what
the LORD says to the men of Judah** and to Jerusalem "Break
up your unplowed ground and do not sow among thorns.
Circumcise yourselves to the LORD, circumcise your hearts, you
men of Judah and people of Jerusalem, or my wrath will break
out and burn like fire because of the evil you have done—burn
with no one to quench it." (Jer. 4:1–4, author emphasis)

Heart drift.

You don't ask someone to *return to me* unless they have wandered.
You also don't ask someone to be "truthful" if they have a track record
of honesty. Another thing you don't do is lay blame on one group if
it's *everyone's* responsibility. Once again it is the lead engine of the men
leading all other connected groups off the cliff. Small talk is definitely
over as God Himself calls the men back from culture to covenant, from
idols to faithfulness, and from insincerity to sincerity of commitment.
He asks for three specific things from His men:

1. Heart Shift (break up your unplowed ground)
2. Energy Shift (do not sow among thorns)
3. Commitment Shift (circumcise yourselves)
4. Loyalty Shift (circumcise your hearts)

In an agrarian society every Jewish man understood what breaking up unplowed ground implied—hard work, discomfort, and sweat.
Similarly, every Jewish man understood
that it is foolish and unproductive to plant
crops and sow good seed among thorns.
And lastly, every Jewish man *most certainly*
understood the concept and practice of
circumcision. As they tore away from their
covenant identity and embraced the practices and gods of the cultures around them,
the "unplowed ground" was the hard con-

> Every Jewish
> man most
> certainly
> understood
> the concept
> and practice of
> circumcision.

dition of their hearts to God that needed to become soft and receptive to the seeds of His love, truth, and words. The admonition not to "sow among thorns" represents the wasted investment of energy pursuing paths of fulfillment in the culture rather than through their covenant relationship with God. Circumcision was a sign physically and spiritually that, as a man, you have a different spiritual identity which calls you to a different life responsibility. Physically, it is an outward sign of an inward marking by God. But in this case God is asking for an inner work and an outer, literal, physical separation of his men from all influences that diminish their connection to Him. He knew how to talk to men meaningfully and in a masculine context so that the men *get it*. God is modeling how all pastors should speak to men in the congregation and notice that He speaks to everybody in the context of speaking to the men. He goes to the source. He knows if He resonates with them and moves their commitment in the right direction everyone connected with them will be pulled that way.

He does it intentionally and without apology.

Jeremiah, for his part, thinks the whole mess with God's people is a fluke and that if he can just talk to the men of Group 1 he will have the problem solved quickly.

> I thought, "These are only the poor; they are foolish, for they do not know the way of the LORD, the requirements of their God. So I will go to the leaders and speak to them; surely they know the way of the LORD, the requirements of their God." But with one accord they too had broken off the yoke and torn off the bonds. Therefore a lion from the forest will attack them, a wolf from the desert will ravage them, a leopard will lie in wait near their towns to tear to pieces any who venture out, for their rebellion is great and their backslidings many. (Jer. 5:4–6)

The men, as a community, had detached themselves from covenant *(broken off the yoke)* and abandoned all responsibility *(torn off the bonds)* because they were, as Jeremiah reports a few verses later, engaged deeply with a sexualized culture and its practices. This direction spiritually spread like an aggressive virus to every segment of society across all strata and each gender—a spirit of self-gratification producing a desensitization to God. The whole community of faith is now leaderless, polluted, and vulnerable to attack according to the covenant of Moab.

The irony is that covenant men then and churched men now are not far apart.

> The irony is that covenant men then and churched men now are not far apart.

God's Glasses

"The men of Judah are the garden of his delight." (Isa. 5:7)

That revelation changes things. The idea that God models delighting in men and tracking them closely convicts me personally and burdens me deeply for the local church worldwide. But even stronger feelings should surface when you consider God checking in your specific "garden of his delight" and pondering: *What does He see reflected in the character the men? Do I even know what's happening on a deep level with the men of my church?* As students of the Bible, it appears either we have missed that modeling, choose to ignore it, or just don't know how to apply what we see. The good news is that thousands of pastors and churches are encountering the Sleeping Giant revelation and response process and deciding *to respond* to what God has shown them about Himself and His attitude toward men.

Leaving the Old Testament, we are left with this: Follow the men and follow the true health of God's people on earth—at least that is God's point of observation and pattern of action. In a world where making distinctions or not giving equal influence to both genders makes you extreme, the Scripture holds steady through the storms of debate to assign both centrality and responsibility to God's men as carriers of His mantle among His people. That's the revelation.

Group 1 then is *still* Group 1 today.

Key Learnings: Where Have All My Good Men Gone?

God to Ezekiel

> Then the Spirit lifted me up and brought me to the gate of the house of the LORD that faces east. There at the entrance to the gate were **twenty-five men**, and I saw among them Jaazaniah son of Azzur and Pelatiah son of Benaiah, leaders of the people. The LORD said to me, **"Son of man, these are the men who are plotting evil and giving wicked advice in this city."** (Ezek. 11:1–2, author emphasis)

> **See how each of the princes of Israel who are in you uses his power to shed blood.** (Ezek. 22:6, author emphasis)

> **I looked for a man among them who would build up the wall and stand before me in the gap on behalf of the land so I would not have to destroy it, but I found none.** So I will pour out my wrath on them and consume them with my fiery anger, bringing down on their own heads all they have done, declares the Sovereign LORD." (Ezek. 22:30–31, author emphasis)

Daniel to God

> I prayed to the Lord my God and confessed: "O Lord, the great and awesome God, who keeps his covenant of love with all who love him and obey his commands, we have sinned and done wrong. We have been wicked and have rebelled; we have turned away from your commands and laws. **We have not listened to your servants the prophets, who spoke in your name to our kings, our princes and our fathers, and to all the people of the land.**" (Dan. 9:4–6, author emphasis)

God to Hosea

Judah's leaders are like those who move boundary stones. I will pour out my wrath on them like a flood of water. (Hos. 5:10, author emphasis)

Like Adam, they have broken the covenant—they were unfaithful to me there. Gilead is **a city of wicked men**, stained with footprints of blood. (Hos. 5:7–8, author emphasis)

God Through Amos

Woe to you who are complacent in Zion, and to you who feel secure on Mount Samaria, you **notable men of the foremost nation, to whom the people of Israel come!** (Amos 6:1, author emphasis)

God through Micah

What misery is mine! I am like one who gathers summer fruit at the gleaning of the vineyard; there is no cluster of grapes to eat, none of the early figs that I crave. The godly have been swept from the land; **not one upright man remains.** All men lie in wait to shed blood; each hunts his brother with a net. Both hands are skilled in doing evil; the ruler demands gifts, the judge accepts bribes, the powerful dictate what they desire— they all conspire together. (Micah 7:1–3, author emphasis)

God through Zephaniah

Her officials are roaring lions, **her rulers** are evening wolves, who leave nothing for the morning. **Her prophets** are arrogant; they are **treacherous men. Her priests** profane the sanctuary and do violence to the law. (Zeph. 3:3–4, author emphasis)

God through Malachi

He will sit as a refiner and purifier of silver; he will purify the Levites and refine them like gold and silver. **Then the LORD will have men who will bring offerings in righteousness.** (Mal. 3:3, author emphasis)

Chapter 8

Forceful Movement, Forceful Men

"From the days of John the Baptist until now, the kingdom of God is advancing forcefully, and forceful men lay hold of it."

MATTHEW 11:12

"Hold on!"

The river was flowing at *five million cubic feet of water per second* and looked completely different than it did the previous summer when I rafted it with guys from church. The main difference was the color— it was almost completely white! Volume, terrain change, and *rate of advance* will do that. The Southern California Basin had received thirty-nine inches of precipitation during the winter months, bringing record snowfall to the mountains. With my heart in my throat, I was trying to navigate the class-five rapids the resulting melt-off snow was producing on the upper Kern River.

"Forward!"

Our instructor warned us that we would be "taking on the Kern" which meant, in order to survive it, we had to attack it. There is no such thing as "finessing" class-five rapids, only attacking. This posture involves pointing your raft at tall rapids and hitting them head-on multiple times during the "run" in order to make it through certain

95

sections of the river. Practically, the command "forward" meant every-one in the raft would shift from directional paddling to all-out *forward* strokes in anticipation of a tall rapid that needed to be speared versus avoided. It's one of the eeriest and most exciting feelings I have ever felt.

You are advancing within something that is constantly advancing.

The weather phenomenon that caused so much rain to fall and, subsequently, so much snow to melt and water to flow downriver in my story is called "El Niño." Warm waters near the equator in the Pacific Ocean trigger major climatic shifts in the weather pattern dropping abnormally large amounts of rain on Southern California. Whenever we have what is called an "El Niño Condition," all sorts of actions and reactions are occurring in the water cycle.

Think about that for a minute and then consider that "El Niño" also means the Christ Child. The birth of a baby boy in the hills outside Bethlehem triggers a surge of spiritual activity that earth never has and never will witness again. God's "El Niño" triggered a redemptive downpour of the kingdom of God that had been building up since the fall. With the advent of "El Niño," all the prophecies and promises that had accumulated for centuries were now melting rapidly, coalescing, and forming an unstoppable river of salvation and transformation from God that Scripture says will not stop advancing until He appears again. Its waters are white with power.

"And forceful men lay hold of it."

When we enter the New Testament discussion of God's pattern and purpose with men, a whole new dimension is present that far exceeds any of our previous observations. The time for "one off" men's ministry is over: no more messengers, burning bushes, songs about vineyards, or old covenant pressures. We only have to look at "El Niño." The revelation is now *God Himself.* The priority and responsibility of inviting men to participate in this powerful advance of the kingdom is convicting in its power and simplicity.

> Jesus models.
> Jesus messages.
> Jesus mentors.

Jesus models. Jesus messages. Jesus mentors.

Show-How

"A student is not above his teacher, but everyone who is fully trained will be like his teacher." (Luke 6:40)

Jesus started with men.

When you read or hear those words, it's easy to be offended. Try not to let competing voices dumb it down, rationalize it, or justify another path to church building that considers your church culture over the Messiah's method for just a second. It would be easy to retreat at this point in the discussion because we know that we are called to disciple everybody. Jesus knew this too, so we are all in the same boat. *However,* tactically Jesus narrowed His focus and energy to the one strategy that would achieve the best results for the kingdom, reach the most people, and create the healthiest expression of His church. The breadth and width created by the numbers coming required the depth and substance of leadership to move it forward productively. His church would need leaders so He had to *fully train* men from His own ranks to ensure the quality.

Job one: *Start calling men and fully train them.*

When planting Saddleback Church, my pastor Rick Warren created a strategy around reaching a guy named "Saddleback Sam." A detailed profile was created that defined who the "hard target" of our church was, how he thought, what his interests were, where his energies were going, what his relationships demanded of him, and what real-life issues were creating headaches for him. The guiding philosophy for us was that *if we built the church to reach women, we would lose the men,* but if we built our strategy around winning and helping men, we would both reach and attract the women, children, and *other new men.* Interestingly,

> If we build our strategy around winning and helping men, we would both reach and attract the women, children, and *other new men.*

nothing about this appeared chauvinistic or macho or politically incorrect. It made perfect sense, and we had the research to back up the strategy. To this end, I credit Rick for aggressively applying the strategy but not for originating the strategy.

Credit Jesus for that.

In his classic work *The Master Plan of Evangelism,* author Robert Coleman meticulously and convincingly lays out the following pattern and progression of Jesus with men.[20]

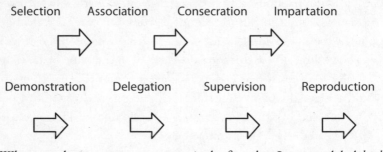

Selection   Association   Consecration   Impartation

Demonstration   Delegation   Supervision   Reproduction

What stands out to me as a pastor is the fact that Jesus modeled *both* a public ministry to large numbers of people *and* a private leader-making ministry to a small group of men in the midst of public ministry. Before we move on, we have to observe the connection: *He used one as a tool to do the other.*

Public Ministry to Masses	Private Mission with Men
Public Meetings	Personal Communion with Father
Everybody	Personal Conversations with Men
Public Preaching	Selected Men
Public Healings	Private Mentoring
Educational Teaching	Experiential Training
Low Requirement (Believe)	High Commitment (Self-Denial)
Three Years	Twenty Centuries
Great Commandment	Great Commission

We call Jesus' way of doing men's ministry the "show-how" method, which is highly intentional and relational. The message to men in this process *from the start* is:

1. I do, you watch.
2. We do together.
3. You do, I watch.
4. YOU do.

Public and planned ministry is happening at the same time private modeling, messaging, and mentoring is going on. The call from the leader feels a lot like this: *"'Come, follow me,' Jesus said, 'and I will make you fishers of men'" (Matt. 4:19).* It reflects the trifecta of the Sleeping Giant revelation: the *priority* of men to our Lord, the *process* and the *product.* Jesus called men into the kingdom enterprise, connected with them in the context of an ongoing public ministry and communicated the tribal knowledge of the kingdom's ins and outs. The integrity and simplicity of Jesus' public-private model is convicting and compelling. It feels so organic and easy to engage. It has a transcendent purpose for where the process is taking men. The personal invitation and investment He has in the men and their mentoring makes it sticky. More important, Jesus knew His process would get Him the product.

Key word: *sticky.*

Many churches are good at the public ministry to men. Men's calendar of events and gatherings include weekend retreats, pancake breakfasts, recovery groups, service opportunities within the church, and other affinity groups of men who share a common interest in sport or hobby. These funnels draw men initially, but they usually run out of gas because there is no larger vision beyond the "gathering" that connects them directly to the mission of the church in a compelling way. As time passes, men's ministry becomes nothing more than bulletin announcements and arbitrary tasks which translate to the men as: *"this is good for you; you should do this if you are a man."* When it comes

> Jesus knew His process would get Him the product.

to this stage, nothing separates this appeal from all the other competing requests for a man's time and energy. The big nets that are cast in hopes of drawing the men are good once or twice; but with no vision or transcendent connection as a part of the process, they lack stickiness and dissolve. Guys "get in" for time, and then they "get out."

Other churches build their men's ministry around high-commitment, semiprivate discipleship processes that communicate strength but do not have wide participation. They are open to all the men of the church, but there is no "come and see" aspect to these kinds of programs. Instead, it's a "come and die" message right out of the box that is communicated either directly by the personalities involved or by the program requirements in terms of homework or time commitment. The perception among the men looking at this from the outside is that these programs are only for men who are biblically literate (on command) and have all their ducks in a row when it comes to sin management, marriage, and ministry. Again, it's the *perception* which may or may not reflect the reality; but because men are deeply afraid of being exposed as unknowledgeable or struggling with personal issues, they self-select out of these groups without even checking into them. The sad part of it all is that the majority of men in the church would *love* to get to a place of high spiritual integrity, but the starting point in their minds is too high a bar. The high-commitment guys then become a "bless me" club that is perceived by the men of the church to be ultraexclusive.

The missing link: *the journey.*

A great event is only as good as the vision behind all the energy and expense. A high-commitment discipleship program is good if a few make it all the way to the end. But it's infinitely better if your events that are gathering men well also cast a vision of leader development and provide a "feeder" for the life and leader development offered in your core discipleship program. This linkage and connectivity of the "getting in" pieces of men's ministry to the "getting healthy, strong, and going" phases is the difference between what we call *unintentional* versus *intentional* men's ministry. Working with churches all over the world, we have discovered that most of them, if they are investing at all in the men, are doing one and not the other. The results are predictable. Check out our breakdown of church practice and see if you can you guess which one is the dominant style.

Unintentional Picture	Intentional Picture
No end game	Begins with the end in mind
No ministry plan/objectives	Has a ministry plan/objectives
No spiritual goals for the man	Specific outcomes identified
No pathway for a man	Defined pathway for a man
No leader development strategy	Leader development structure
No visible champion	Visible leader
Men connected to events	Men connected to a small group
Public events seen as primary	Public events part of a pathway
Results:	**Results:**
Shallow	Depth
Lots of fits and restarts	Consistency of culture
Emotional highs and lows	Confidence of identity
Disconnected leadership	Connected leaders
Low participation churchwide	High participation churchwide
Making impressions	Making disciples
Analogy: Like a movie.	Analogy: Like a virus.
Go. Sit. Listen. Watch. It's over.	Catch it. Get infected.
Go back to your life.	Infect others.

Hopefully, you were evaluating your own church as you looked down the columns describing intentional versus unintentional. The good news is that if you are wanting to move from the column on the left over to the column on the right just keep reading. We are going to take you through the process of going from unintentional to intentional in the next section. But for now we just want you to clearly see that Jesus

> Whatever Jesus models for us in Scripture is meant for us.

practiced *intentional men's ministry.* Then we want you to draw the right conclusion: *whatever Jesus models for us in Scripture is meant for us.*

He showed us exactly how.

Having fully trained his core leaders, it was now time to wake the Sleeping Giant through Peter and the eleven in Jerusalem as well as reach the Gentile world through reaching men in every culture. But how?

Pentecost's High-Value Targets

First-century Jerusalem during the Feast of Pentecost.

Jews from all over the known world are descending on your city. Imagine you are a Jewish man. The predominant thinking of your upbringing leads you to one thought as you walk the streets: *Thank God I am not a woman, a child, or a Gentile.* It's a good time to be a man. The air is thick with chauvinism, narcissism, and nationalism though, for you, it's called being a man. And then, like now, it creates a lot of suffering and marginalizes large segments of the population in the name of broken male culture. You say, "Good thing we got rid of that criminal from Nazareth who was calling himself King of the Jews. He was spotted talking to and defending women, inviting children to share the same space as men, and telling stories about Samaritans that make them appear civilized. His followers seemed to have disappeared as well. Oh well, this is Jerusalem: another year, another false Messiah, right. What's going on over there? Who *are* those guys? What are they babbling? Maybe they should lay off the wine? And who's this group all standing to attention like they are going to break into song?"

> Then Peter stood up with the Eleven, raised his voice and addressed the crowd: "Fellow Jews and all of you who live in Jerusalem, let me explain this to you; listen carefully to what I say. **These men are not drunk**, as you suppose. It's only nine in the morning!" (Acts 2:14–15, author emphasis)

You ask, "Is the ringleader of this group talking to the men?"

Men of Israel, listen to this: Jesus of Nazareth was a man accredited by God to you by miracles, wonders and signs, which God did among you through him, as you yourselves know. (Acts 2:22, author emphasis)

"That answers that," you say. "Why does he keep hammering the men? He keeps saying 'Brothers' and 'Rulers and elders of the people!' Whoa! Look at all those guys stepping forward."

The rest of the story?

They seized Peter and John, and because it was evening, they put them in jail until the next day. But many who heard the message believed, and **the number of men grew to about five thousand.** (Acts 4:3–4, author emphasis)

The story of the birth of the church is the story of the waking up of the sons of covenant (Jewish men) and introducing them anew as sons of Christ. The Holy Spirit chooses His targets carefully, borrows Peter's mouth, and starts firing polished arrows of gospel hope and fulfillment into one male heart after another. Once pierced, He then proceeds to fill and form Jewish men who now begin to act strangely inclusive, compassionate, and accepting of the same people who for centuries they have marginalized in the name of religion or misplaced nationalism. Everyone is astonished by their transformation of character and conduct all in the span of a day or two. There *is no other explanation—only God Himself could turn broken male culture on its head like that!* The witness of transformed men is unequivocal and thousands more come to Christ from all segments of society. Both the celebration and persecution of Jesus through Christians are just getting started. Jewish men begin to relieve pain versus cause it. They start reducing loads versus creating burdens. They are raising spirits versus crushing them. They are reaching souls versus remaining soulless.

> The Holy Spirit chooses His targets carefully.

> The world was brought by God to Jerusalem to see men filled, formed, and transformed before their eyes.

The church is born but so is the first justice movement ever.

In the first century the world was brought by God to Jerusalem to see men filled, formed, and transformed before their eyes. The reaction? A massive harvest of souls and the beginning burst of the Great Commandment and the Great Commission moving outward to every nation. Today the world can see a movement the instant one erupts digitally within minutes of its public inception. And just as the world watched men, who, for centuries thought and behaved one way, transform before their eyes by the power of God's Spirit, so today God is preparing a similar witness and harvest through His men transforming and touching others' hearts through the local church. In every tongue and on every continent, sons of culture will become sons of Christ, bringing a witness of God's power and an outpouring of God's justice. The pattern and purpose of God for men will prevail once again in His church. The church will be glorified in its completion in the same fashion of its inception.

With a masculine eruption of spiritual transformation.

The Rest of the Story

The story of God choosing to birth the church strategically through the reaching, filling, forming, and witness of transformed men should speak directly to all pastors hoping to win congregational health and community witness. It makes perfect sense theologically and functionally. The Spirit of the Lord was upon Jesus to bring God's justice to people affected by the broken male culture of the day. People who, because of centuries of cultural masculinity, were abused, labeled, used, marginalized, and robbed of dignity. Then the man of aggressive compassion, justice, and righteousness arrived and stood in the gap between the men who brought suffering and their victims. The physically unacceptable, morally unacceptable, ethnically unacceptable, and socially unwelcomed or unacceptable found their champion. Jesus broke all the rules of broken male culture. The men filled with His Spirit at Pentecost did the same.

The kingdom came.

This boldness attracted the masses and won over the consciences of the most skeptical. These men were also heavily persecuted as their power to transcend culture threatened those tethered by pride and insecurity to the same. But the church grew, women and children saw new men and new wine controlling their actions, and justice started coming to communities all over the world in a new way through God's men versus more of the same. More important, the God who watches, tracks, and loves justice was pleased.

This movement was promised and purposed to explode outward from Jerusalem to the world. But who would God choose? Why would He choose him? And would the pattern of movement through men continue?

Now for the rest of the story.

God's Chosen Instrument

> The Lord told him, "Go to the house of Judas on Straight Street and ask for a man from Tarsus named Saul, for he is praying. In a vision he has seen a man named Ananias come and place his hands on him to restore his sight." "Lord," Ananias answered, "I have heard many reports about this man and all the harm he has done to your saints in Jerusalem. And he has come here with authority from the chief priests to arrest all who call on your name." But the Lord said to Ananias, **"Go! This man is my chosen instrument to carry my name before the Gentiles and their kings and before the people of Israel.** (Acts 9:11–15, author emphasis)

Saul's misplaced energy and ego, now under the control of the Holy Spirit, gets redirected by God to secure the Gentile world for Christ. He becomes God's man for the nations.

A Men's Small Group Meeting Sparks a Missions Movement

In the church at Antioch there were prophets and teachers: Barnabas, Simeon called Niger, Lucius of Cyrene, Manaen (who had been brought up with Herod the tetrarch) and Saul. While they were worshiping the Lord and fasting, the Holy Spirit said, "Set apart for me Barnabas and Saul for the work to which I have called them." So after they had fasted and prayed, they placed their hands on them and sent them off. (Acts 13:1–3)

Reflections of Psalm 133 are present here. The oil of God's presence falling upon brothers worshipping in unity: "For there the LORD bestows his blessing, even life forevermore" (Ps. 133:3). God calls out of a men's small group at the church in Antioch the world's first missionaries for Christ. We need to see the dynamic of men connecting and God calling out men *as they connect*.

Paul's "Show How" Pattern

He came to Derbe and then to Lystra, where a disciple named Timothy lived, whose mother was a Jewess and a believer, but whose father was a Greek. The brothers at Lystra and Iconium spoke well of him. **Paul wanted to take him along on the journey**, so he circumcised him because of the Jews who lived in that area, for they all knew that his father was a Greek. As they traveled from town to town, they delivered the decisions reached by the apostles and elders in Jerusalem for the people to obey. **So the churches were strengthened in the faith and grew daily in numbers.** (Acts 16:1–3, author emphasis)

> We need to see the dynamic of men connecting and God calling out men as they connect.

Silas, Luke, Mark, Titus, Timothy, Epaphrus, Tychicus, Onesimus, and Erastus were among the men Paul fully trained; and they, too, became like their teacher planting the first churches all over the Mediterranean. He simply took men *"along the journey."*

Focusing Uniquely on the Sleeping Giant

> We proclaim Him, admonishing **every man** and teaching **every man** with all wisdom, so that we may present **every man** complete in Christ. **For this purpose also I labor**, striving according to His power, which mightily works within me. (Col. 1:28–29 NASB, author emphasis)

Paul understood the power and promise of men as well as the need to take advantage of their energies and expression. The great apostle did not want to waste any effort, so he directed his energy toward the intentional proclamation of Christ to men, followed by the admonition, education, presentation, and completion of those same men in the Lord. Eventually, he released these men to lead the early church all over the Mediterranean. This is the same man who, upon reflection, summarized the power of one man: *"For just as through the disobedience of the one man the many were made sinners, so also through the obedience of the one man the many will be made righteous" (Rom. 5:19).* The great apostle saw biblically so he prioritized tactically and moved intentionally, without apology, to grow the church exponentially.

The result: the kingdom was advancing forcefully through forceful men as Jesus predicted.

The Sleeping Giant prediction by Jesus portended the promise and potential of a small group of fully trained men who became like Him and, in becoming like Him, became forceful men who would be used to advance the kingdom. In order to achieve over twenty centuries of church movement, God decided that three years, twelve guys, and the indwelling power and leadership from the Holy Spirit would cover it. Reexamining this linkage is mission

> God decided that three years, twelve guys, and the indwelling power and leadership from the Holy Spirit would cover it.

critical to the present condition and future health of the church locally and globally. Hear me: the hope of the world is the local church and the *untapped hope of the local church right now is its men.*

The revelation now demands a response.

Key Learnings

- The power of men comes from God's own revelation to man and requires great responsibility and response from men.
- The advance of the church will come from Jesus' own example and strategy.
- Godly men moving within an intentional process will produce life transformation and leader multiplication just as Jesus modeled.
- The "come and see" message will precede the "come and die" to fuel the engine of future leadership.
- Intentional men's ministry beats accidental men's ministry every time.
- Broken male culture leads to suffering and marginalization of others in the culture.
- God's redemptive plan can turn this phenomenon around as demonstrated in Acts.
- Fully trained men, mentored by the well-discipled for the Lord's purpose are the key to transforming today's church.

Chapter 9

Step 1: Strong Vision and Mission

The LORD said to Moses: "Bring me seventy of Israel's elders who are known to you as leaders and officials among the people. Have them come to the Tent of Meeting, that they may stand there with you. I will come down and speak with you there, and I will take of the Spirit that is on you and put the Spirit on them. They will help you carry the burden of the people so that you will not have to carry it alone."

NUMBERS 11:16–17

It's called the "Magic Wand" meeting.

The ingredients of a successful Magic Wand meeting include the following:

- One roomful of pastors and me
- Strong feelings about the need to activate their men
- Ideas relating to what they would like to see happen
- Awareness of problems that could be solved by spiritually healthy men
- Willingness to build a life and leader development pathway

- Church initiatives that could benefit from male energy and expression
- Leadership needs in the church
- One large whiteboard to write everything down
- *One question* that ignites the discussion

If you had a magic wand and could "zap" the men's culture in your church, what would happen?

To help the group along, we lead them with some "for example" prompts to get the ball rolling. "For example:"

1. What new behaviors would you see?
2. How would their relationships change?
3. What would their spiritual life look like?
4. How would they see themselves in the context of church?
5. What would the community impact be?
6. How would their church involvement change?
7. What would the men's culture feel like?
8. What kind of man would it attract?
9. How would it benefit the man?
10. What results would be nonnegotiable?
11. How would it impact the other ministries of the church?
12. How would church health be affected?

Having conducted so many Magic Wand meetings, we have constructed a Sleeping Giant whiteboard here that captures many of the most common responses.

The Magic Wand Whiteboard		
If you had a magic wand and could "zap" the men's culture in your church, what would happen? **"Our men would be _____ (fill in the blank) _____."**		
Connected to other men	Defeating temptations	Generous givers
Men of the Word	Sharing their faith	Supporting other ministries
Men of the Spirit	Men of prayer	Blessing the community
Great husbands	Behind vision of senior pastor	Helping the poor
Great dads	Making disciples	Planting needed ministries
More responsible	Spiritual leaders in homes	Leading small groups
Serving in the church	Coaching small group leaders	Helping pastor the people
Impacting the marketplace	An actionable network	Changing the world
Standing against injustice	Tithers	Reaching the broken
Donating skill sets to church	Trained for ministry	Fighting evil everywhere

Once the board is full, every pastor has had his chance to hold the magic wand, and each has verbalized his dream for the men, we then tell them two things. First, we say, "Whatever you build for your men going forward must accomplish those things (the stuff on the whiteboard) in the lives of your men." Second, we say, "You need to do this

exact process that we have done with you *with your men.*" You might be
wondering: *Why do they make them go through this process?* Or, *Why do
they strongly encourage them to do the same process with their leaders?* The
answer to this highlights the importance of Step 1 in the Sleeping Giant
process. We want them to begin painting the target. We want them to build a God-sized dream. We want them to always begin with the *end in mind.* We want them to tell us what they think is missing. We want them to be fully vested. We want them to begin the process of creating meaningful mission and vision. We want them to have personal buy-in and "skin in the game," as they say. We want them to tell us what they want. We want the thing that has been bugging them on the inside to come out. We want them to look in the mirror and evaluate their own lives against these same markers. In the process of making them articulate what they want to see happen, we are able to unearth answers to several other important questions at the same time. Questions like:

> We want them to begin painting the target. We want them to build a God-sized dream.

1. What *unresolved problems* will a strong men's community help solve?
2. Is there a sense of *urgency*?
3. What *pervasive problems* are your men facing?
4. How will men's ministry *address those problems*?
5. Who will this effort with men and solution *impact directly*? Who is in the immediate blast zone of this expression?
6. What do you see as *deficient* about what you are offering now?
7. What is going to *resonate* with men?
8. How will the church realize a *tangible value*?
9. What results will men *personally* experience?
10. What do you see as *meaningful* ministry to men?
11. How healthy are the *men's leaders themselves*?

These are the questions breakthrough men's ministries in the local church answer *before they do anything.* If there is one common denominator among churches who are failing to meaningfully reach men and build a leader engine for their pastor, it's this: *they don't know what the target is!*

Step 1: clearly define the mission and vision of your men's ministry.

Making a Statement

If people can't see what God is doing, they stumble all over themselves; But when they attend to what he reveals, they are most blessed. (Prov. 29:18 MSG)

I remember taking my church training team for Every Man out to Palm Springs, California. We were going to be there for forty-eight hours to come up with two statements. The first was going to be our mission statement, and the second was our vision statement. Our ministry had evolved. This meant we needed to pray, fast, and seek the Lord for what He was calling us to be *now*. Our founding mission was titanic: *a worldwide church-to-church movement of men*. Sounded great but it didn't paint the target for us very well because it was too broad to have any personal meaning for the team, our users, or our supporters. Whatever we came up with had to be consistent with the original vision but had to expand and define it *dynamically*.

After filling pages of flip charts and asking tons of questions, we came up with two mission and vision statements. But then we had to put those through a filtering process to get to the true essence of our ministry, the mission God was calling us to, and the vision of how we were going to achieve it. More tough questions, more prayer, and more scrutiny got us to our goal, and in the end everyone felt that we had discerned the Lord's mission and vision for the future. What follows are a mission statement and a vision statement that have guided us for the last decade, steered us through the many storms, shaped everything, and are guiding us right now. We share it as a testimony and as just one example for you to see as we explore Step 1 of the Sleeping Giant process.

Our Vision
The vision of Every Man Ministries is:
to revolutionize men's ministry
to free men spiritually
and to empower spiritual health worldwide.

Our Mission
The mission of Every Man Ministries is to help men
Get In   Get Healthy   Get Strong   Get Going

Here are a few reasons why having a vision and mission for your men's community is critical. It:

1. Defines what could be.
2. Motivates people internally.
3. Draws everyone forward.
4. Defines your core priorities.
5. Rallies resources.
6. Creates purpose.
7. Defines the process.
8. Provides common language.
9. Defines how we serve others.
10. Unites energy and expression toward concrete goals.

Now you know why vision and mission statements are more than words or a framed showpiece in the conference room. Properly thought through, these statements of purpose and practice become the guiding force for *everything*. From the people you bring into the ministry, to the programming you offer, to the way you feel about what you do. A good vision and mission invites stakeholders (your men, in this case) in the kingdom enterprise to ask: *What must I do to make sure that happens?* It also gets them volunteering their time without your having to nag or harass them to show up. They are eager to participate because the vision is strong. Similarly, for the men you reach and serve, it sends a clear message that you care about them. This is where the church could learn a thing or two from organizations that try to understand and serve the customer in a world-class way versus assume people will swallow poor vision and mission because it's assumed under the banner and authority of the "church." In a world where excellence is expected on so many levels, it is mind-boggling how so many men's ministries in the local church thrive on and accept mediocrity as they minister to men. What they don't get is that they will only get *one chance* to make a good first impression.

> Men don't like to associate with things that don't reflect strength, excellence, and quality.

Hear us: it's not that men don't want to participate in the men's ministry; it's that they don't like to associate with things that don't reflect strength, excellence, and quality. A men's ministry that knows why it is there is living out its mission and vision and shows that it is committed to it is the first test. The Every Man mission and vision, for example, communicates what we feel we owe the churches we serve and the men we help. What's that, you say? Four things:

1. A clear vision
2. Deep relationships
3. Intentional leader development
4. Spiritual health

These are the same four core values every men's ministry owes to their senior pastor and the men it serves in the local church. If those things are not deeply imbedded in the leaders and in the culture, do not expect the commitment, energy, fraternity, productivity, and transformations that accompany these four factors when they are present.

Creating A New Canvas

Forget the former things; do not dwell on the past. See, I am doing a new thing! Now it springs up; do you not perceive it? I am making a way in the desert and streams in the wasteland. (Isa. 43:18–19)

Etch A Sketch.

This was the name of a magnetic drawing board I had as a toy when I was little. It was the iPad of its time for children and adults who couldn't contain their creative impulses. This thick red tablet had a milky white screen with two small knobs that moved a black magnetic line up, down, and side to side. If you were really adept with the knobs, you could create curving lines (something I never mastered) and some amazing pictures. The thing about drawing with an Etch A Sketch was that it was one continuous line. There was no stopping and placing the cursor in a new location on the screen, which created issues. The main one being: What do I do when I want to start fresh? *Answer:* When using the Etch A Sketch, all I had to do was pick up the tablet, turn it upside down, and then flip it right side up again. Voila!

A new canvas.

After walking hundreds of churches through the Sleeping Giant process, we have discovered that many times it's hard to stop something once you have started it, *even if it is not working.* Maybe your church is like this when it comes to men's ministry. You launched a meeting, a group, or a Bible study for men, and the attendance and energy were strong initially. Men's launches experience a healthy beginning (especially if the senior pastor is involved), but over time it diminishes in size, energy, and effectiveness because it lacks the one thing that sustains all movements—a vision bigger than the meeting itself. We have discovered that churches in this situation are now caught between a rock and a hard place. The rock is this: the men who have become the "regulars" really enjoy this meeting, the fellowship, and the connection. The hard place is: there is no larger vision for the gathering of men that helps the church raise up leaders, attract new men, or drive core initiatives. Our message to those churches, and possibly to you, is simple.

Time to *Etch A Sketch.*

This is exactly what I had to do when I was asked to assume the

> It's hard to stop something once you have started it, even if it is not working.

leadership of the men's ministry after being a volunteer leader. We had various men's groups meeting in different places on campus, each addressing different subjects. We had regular men's breakfasts catering to another segment of men in the church. We had a men's wilderness ministry that had its own committee and leadership team. We had an annual retreat where another group of men would gather for a weekend. We had a Promise Keeper's Bible study, sexual integrity, and a marriage group as well. We also had a service organization that began out of a men's retreat called Men of Impact. The men in these groups were just doing what the church structure permitted and allowed them to do.

> The grand irony of all this activity was that none of the energy was intentionally supporting the vision and mission of our church.

Nobody was the wiser.

The good news was that there was a lot of energy on the part of men to get together, fellowship, and be God's man. But the bad news was that all these ministries were competing against one another for the same audience, competing for calendar, competing for budget, competing for announcements on the weekend, and competing for space in the weekend program. The grand irony of all this activity *among the men of our church* was that none of the energy was *intentionally supporting the vision and mission of our church* in a tangible way. It was a classic example of *unintentional* men's ministry. No end game. No larger objective to help the church. No leader development strategy. No spiritual pathway. No connection to our small groups strategy. Indirectly, men's ministry was in direct competition with the church's strategy without the church being aware of it!

After interviewing hundreds of pastors for this book, I (Kenny) have found that I was not alone. Many shared how they were not big supporters of men's ministry because the men in those ministries did not have the interests of the church in mind at all. The church, according to these pastors, was the space provider, logistics coordinator, registration center, and back office support for all of these men's ministry enterprises and efforts. One of these pastors, leading one of the largest congregations in his state, came up to me after hearing me speak and said, *"I was going to officially cancel all things related to men's ministry just last week. There was no value at all coming back to the church in any tangible way that I could detect. But one of my guys went to your training in California and told me that you told him to take me to coffee and ask me this question: 'What has God called you to do, and how can men's ministry get behind what God has called you to do?' I could not believe it, and that was God's way of telling me not to get rid of men's ministry but to change the model."*

We will talk more about the importance of aligning the men's ministry with the vision of the pastor in the next chapter. For now, if you are a men's ministry leader, just know that a pastor's cooperation usually tracks with those ministries that are helping him reach the goals God has set before him. If you are a pastor, don't throw the baby out with the bath water! You have a Sleeping Giant that can be activated and leveraged to drive the mission and vision faster than you ever thought possible. You just need to keep on reading.

Stick with us.

After being handed the men's ministry, I had my first "Magic Wand" meeting of my life with more than thirty men's leaders of our church and one of our pastors. For the first time we began with the end in mind. We had white butcher paper plastered all over the living room with everyone's "zap" of the men's culture at Saddleback Church. Great concepts and ideas flowed. Good energy and healthy angst flowed out of men, investing them powerfully in the coming solution and plan. Deficiencies were exposed and acknowledged. Priorities were assigned. And for the first time, we started talking about the purpose of men's ministry being to support our pastor and *produce leaders* not just good dads, husbands, or Christians as ends in themselves.

Why was this meeting a turning point?

Because we unified around the first versions of a new mission and vision that were bigger than any man's individual study or group or interest. *This* was the direction that would change men's ministry from being the quirky uncle of our church family to a true stakeholder with real influence. In the coming years we had many "funerals" for men's ministries that served only themselves *to the exclusion of* serving the needs of the church. This is an important distinction to make because, as you will learn, if you build it the right way, your men's pathway and process can provide amazing fraternity, develop the man, *and* develop the leader with the church's DNA. That's what a strong men's culture in a church does! But the transition over to intentional men's ministry from unintentional isn't always easy. We weathered the ire and disdain of disaffected men who felt the church's job was to serve them and their group versus the other way around. We won many of these men over, but some could never see past the borders of their own group in order to see the church that is called to fulfill the Great Commission and Great Commandment.

The lesson: *a hard process is worth the product.*

So whether it's an event, a study, or a meeting that you are evaluating, a strong mission and vision help you navigate between "Could we do this?" and "Should we do this?" The answer so often to "Could we do it?" is: *sure you could.* The answer to "Should we do this?" depends on what happens when the opportunity before you collides head-on with your mission and vision because the stronger of the two always wins. That is why step one of the Sleeping Giant process is Step 1. Pray, bring together the right group of men, and grab your wand! Ultimately, we want to discover the "we must do this" opportunities.

> A hard process is worth the product.

It is *mission critical.*

Key Learnings

- You must identify the key issues, challenges, and opportunities you need to address in order to reach and grow the men of your culture.

- This can be discovered not by survey but by interview (talking with the men to hear their hearts). Each will yield different results.
- Think about your desired future. What would that look like for your men's ministry and the church? What is ultimately the target? What is the BIG idea?
- Ownership is key to the success of the mission.
- *Mission* and *vision* must be executable and achievable, not just words. It must vibrantly live in the lives of the men.
- Identify the core values related to the mission and vision.
- One must not be afraid to end what is not supporting the church's mission and risk starting new ways.
- Tap the passion, energy, gifts, and abilities that already exist in your men and direct them toward the target.
- Mission and Vision (defined)
    - Mission: What your ministry is about, how we get to the desired state, what we do. It reflects today.
        - For example: we want to help men get connected to other spiritually healthy men (GET IN) for the purpose of becoming spiritually healthy themselves (GET HEALTHY) so that we can deeply disciple them (GET STRONG) to reach the world for Christ (GET GOING).
    - Vision: Why your ministry exists. What the ministry is to become. The big, God-sized picture. The ultimate goal. Reflects the future.

Chapter 10

Step 2: Strong Alignment with the Pastoral Vision

*Remember your leaders, who spoke the word of God
to you. Consider the outcome of their way of life and
imitate their faith.*

HEBREWS 13:7

"He's gone rogue."

Usually you will encounter this phrase in spy novels when counterintelligence operatives, spies, or assassins leave the "grid" and, consequently, the control of their handlers. In any context the word *rogue* suggests someone or something has become unorthodox, unpredictable, dangerous, or solitary. Practically, that person or group has escaped your control or ability to manage their activities in any functional or positive way. On film or in real life, the response to the news that someone or something has "gone rogue" is the same: "Oh, no" or "Uh-oh." These are the uncolorful and sanitized responses one might hear. The inner reaction is more telling—deep fear. That's because the man or men who have "gone rogue" have either the asset of proximity to things or people you value or tribal knowledge that they can use against their employers or sponsors. What damage they may or may not do with those assets is what makes the "rogue" men ones that need to be feared if they are connected to what you are doing. The feeling is not good.

They make you feel vulnerable to attack from within.

Having consulted for hundreds of churches, we have had countless pastors tell us that the men's ministry in their churches has "gone rogue." Their expression not ours. When a pastor says this, I know immediately that he is saying several things all at once. He means that:

1. Programming or meetings for men are happening in some form.
2. The church has little influence or desires not to have influence over what goes on in those meetings.
3. The men leading those meetings have developed subcongregations within the larger congregation.
4. There is not a connected vision or purpose for those meetings that serves the needs of the church directly.
5. There is a feeling that the men in those groups have become or could become adversarial or a bastion of discontent within that body of believers.
6. There is no real connection or loyalty to the senior pastor or lead pastor to serve him or make him successful in the mission God has called him to achieve.
7. There is a fear that the proximity, tribal knowledge, or connections of the men in those meetings makes confronting or changing the men's ministry over to one that is producing leaders and supporting the pastor fraught with difficulty or egos, *or both.*

> We have had countless pastors tell us that the men's ministry in their churches has "gone rogue."

Rogue.

The Sleeping Giant revelation and response, as well as the process, does not allow for such dysfunction and disunity that is *self-inflicted.* For some churches it is not so much that men's activities have gone rogue but that they do not tie well into the larger infrastructure, planning, and overall discipleship process. Questions are not asked on the front end, and there are no mission, vision, objectives, or strategies to make sure they are achieved. Accidentally and emotionally driven, some guy asked the pastor at some point if he was doing anything for the men, and the overworked and underpaid pastor, who could not add one more responsibility, said: "Well, if you have a heart for that, then *you're it!*" We call this *free-market ministry development,* and it works to a certain point for certain things. Men's ministry is not one of those things you want to let loose organically for long because somewhere along the way it is going to start becoming self-serving versus church-serving. The focus will shift from gathering the men of the church, a feeling of unity and larger purpose, to convening the men to serve their needs for knowledge or help them individually without any bigger reason for their investment of time and energy. The "why" for doing something is not any larger than helping the man be more accountable, a better husband, more moral, a better father, a better man, or a better disciple. All these are not bad reasons to "get in" and might even be the impetus, but they will not sustain something that serves the church in a direct way unless the pastor's vision, needs, and desire to fulfill greater objectives is meaningfully connected to all those relationships and activity in some way.

> The Sleeping Giant revelation and response does not allow for dysfunction and disunity that is *self-inflicted*.

A quantum leap in thinking must occur.

The biggest failing we have seen among men hoping to build and maintain strong men's ministries in the local church is this: it's about the men's ministry being successful versus *serving their pastor and making him succeed*. They forget that God called this man first, that he is the shepherd of the people, that God speaks to him about where he wants to take the body, and that he is in authority over them. He is the leader. He is their leader. We impress on pastors and men's leadership that rogue enterprises would not be tolerated in any other organization which has a stated mission and people who care enough to guard it. In a business or military context, we call it insubordination. But so often in the church

> It's about the men's ministry being successful versus *serving their pastor and making him succeed.*

context we call it men's ministry! That is, men attempting to build a ministry separate from or disconnected from the vision and mission God has appointed a senior or lead pastor to accomplish. The Sleeping Giant process directly connects and keeps reconnecting the success of the men's ministry, its leaders, and those participating in it to the ministry traction it gives a senior or lead pastor.

His success *is success*.

To wake the Sleeping Giant in your church, both the pastor and the men of the church need to *reframe* the other and see the partnership first to realize the powerful advance God wants.

Pastor's Power to Empower

The watchman opens the gate for him, and the sheep listen to his voice. He calls his own sheep by name and leads them out. When he has brought out all his own, he goes on ahead of them, and his sheep follow him because they know his voice. But they will never follow a stranger; in fact, they will run away from him because they do not recognize a stranger's voice. (John 10:3–5)

Indulge me. Men are a lot like my dog Rusty.

Rusty shows up in front of me with his deflated soccer ball in his mouth hoping that I see him, his desire to play, and that I will be willing to engage him. He is so predictable. I can predict with near perfect accuracy when he is going to go get his ball and approach me to play. After we have a "session" of throwing, retrieving, tug-of-war, and wrestling, he is content and doesn't bug me anymore looking for attention that day. The problem is *when I don't engage him.* Since I am the alpha male in the household, Rusty responds differently to me than he does to *everybody* else. We have this unique connection, and he responds to my authority and affection in a way that makes the rest of the family jealous. So when I am gone for a few days doing conferences in churches, he starts to act funny with Chrissy and the kids. That is, he starts to bully them, bark more, and act like he's in charge, ordering people into action with relentless barking until he gets what he wants. My relationship to him, my authority over him, and my ability to motivate him are unique to me. The big lesson is obvious.

Disconnection to him brings destructive tendencies with others in the family.

Men in your congregation show up on the weekend wondering if you see them. They are like Rusty sitting there in front of you. Make no mistake: their tails are wagging, they are full of energy and enthusiasm, but they are not sure if they'll be noticed, ignored, chastised, or dismissed. The game changer for Rusty is when I look at him and say, "Rusty, what are you doing?" That's the cue: *I say his name.* He starts turning in circles and bending low in anticipation of a coming engagement with me. He lives for those words and knows they don't come *all the time* because he would play all day long. That's not going to happen. But a good session every now and then goes a long way to keep him in line.

> When pastors discharge the men to junior staffers or laymen to be *their voice*, the men will start acting out of character.

Make no mistake, pastor, the men in your congregation want the leader of the house to see them, recognize their desire to be integral (versus incidental), and are wondering if you are willing to actually engage them *personally and meaningfully.* They are waiting for you to call out *their name* at some point in a positive and affirming way. The problem is *when you don't engage them.* It's the way God has wired men. You are the alpha male in the household; your men will respond to you a lot differently than they will to *anybody* else in the church from pastors on staff to their wives at home. Senior and lead pastors can have a special and powerful connection to their men if they are intentional and purposeful in the relationship.

They can get their men acting on a simple voice command if there is the perception among the men that you see and value them. They will respond to your authority and overrespond to direct attention and inclusion in a way that makes the rest of the family jealous over their loyalty. But when pastors discharge the men to junior staffers or laymen to be *their voice,* the men will start acting out of character within your congregation or just not activate at all. Instead, they will start to assert themselves in your own house, take liberties, bark more, and act like they are in charge until they get their needs for validation met. Hear us: your relationship to your men, your spiritual authority over your men, and your ability to motivate them are unique to you, pastor. They are a much more critical member to the family than a dog and, as such, a much more impactful force for good or for bad depending on *how they perceive the church is perceiving their value.*

> Your relationship to your men, your spiritual authority over your men, and your ability to motivate them are unique to you.

That is on you.

I know one pastor who gets it and is winning big with his guys with a relatively small but consistent investment. He regularly takes five to ten minutes off the end of his sermons, dismisses the women and kids, and tells the men of the church to come forward to have a meeting with him. That five to ten minutes is gold to his men. He gives them some vision for where the church is headed, a spiritual lesson, or a more personal call to action which he would like them to pray over in the weeks to come. It is a powerful moment for the men of this church every time he does this. They don't know when he is going to do it, but they live for it because it is so meaningful on *so many levels as a man.* He stays on time. He looks them in the eyeball. He makes a spiritual deposit. He sends them out with something in their head, in their hand, and in the heart. When those men reconnect to their families, what do you think the first question is when they start back home? If you guessed "What did Pastor talk to you about?" You are right.

Brilliant.

So what did he accomplish in less than five minutes' time?

1. He calls the men by name.
2. He communicates *tribal knowledge* uniquely meant for them.
3. He cultivates a personal connection to them.
4. He accumulates relational capital to spend later on strategic priorities.
5. He appoints them directly or indirectly to message their families.
6. He saves money, time, and effort.
7. He mobilizes leadership to mobilize the congregation from the inside-out versus from the bulletin or e-mail or announcements.
8. He uses this window to tell them he needs them and points them to the men's leadership pathway, people, and process.
9. He positions them as spiritual leaders in the church.
10. He creates traction and mobility within his people.

Brilliant *and* biblical.

The power of the pastor to empower the men of a church is an untapped vein of gold that expands his relational capital a hundred-fold if he simply knows how to mine and extract it. My own pastor meets with and tells the men of our church what is coming before big initiatives or changes in church direction. He casts vision with us. He laughs with us. He pours into us spiritually. He tells us how vital we are to achieving the goal. He includes and values us in the enterprise.

He points men to the men's network to develop into leaders. He tells the men he needs more leaders to engage. He calls me his "Joab" and directs the men to respond to my leadership. At the end of these meetings, we pray for him. One morning a few times a year is all it costs Pastor Rick, but he knows the return is massive.

> Men want an identity to house their masculinity and are waiting to be used for a kingdom assignment.

The sheep respond aggressively to the voice of *their shepherd*.

Healthy Spiritual Authority

Remember your leaders, who spoke the word of God to you. Consider the outcome of their way of life and imitate their faith. (Heb. 13:7)

Remember and consider.

The opposite of those two words describes the way most men in the church view their pastor's authority in their lives. Instead of strongly remembering and considering it, they *forget* and *ignore* the fact that in God's family there is a structure of spiritual authority that is purposed to move God's purposes forward in their lives and in the church. This approach to their pastor can be intentional, cultural, or adopted out of biblical ignorance. Unmodeled and unmentored, fueled by the consumer spirit of the age, and perpetuated by relationally ambivalent church culture, pastors today fight an uphill battle when trying to build a culture that strikes a biblical balance of community and authority among the men. Some pastors are so panicked over numbers they don't want to offend anyone. Others simply lack the relational capital to give their authority any real meaning. More telling is that the majority of pastors don't have someone they would call "their pastor," someone who is a mentor and spiritual father that is free to speak into their lives with clarity, authority, and authenticity. I have seen healthy churches who possess a healthy balance of community and authority between the pastor and the people. I have also helped churches who lack it.

The difference is stark.

> Most churches do not even know what they are missing because they have been inoculated by imbalance for so long it has become their "normal."

My conclusion after being inside so many church cultures is this: most churches do not even know what they are missing because they have been inoculated by imbalance for so long it has become their "normal." Similarly, churches that have healthy admiration and earned respect for their leader can't fathom existing any other way. In one church culture the men proudly refer to their leader as "my pastor." There is a friendly, warm, and strong loyalty. In the other church culture men refer to their church name first when identifying themselves. In this instance the church functions like a brand, something you wear that says you are on the team; but it doesn't go deeper than that and shouldn't. One reference screams relationship, honor, and connection. The other mutes those and communicates distance, safety, and image.

When you are in one church culture, there is a unity that goes beyond affiliation to personal affection for the pastor and his role in their lives. In the other there is a lot of sincerity, but it lacks the glue-like affinity for the man. This sense of loyalty leaks into the church at every level for better and for worse. It manifests itself in the freedom both the staff and members feel to honor and defend their pastor with each other or complain about and criticize him down through the rank and file. It seeps into the DNA of every ministry and every leader of every ministry. It fosters the creation of rogue men's ministries or squashes them in their tracks. Every pastor would love one, but most settle for the other. One is a team who loves their coach and mentor. The other is a team who tolerates him and plays nice while functionally serving their own agenda and interests.

All you have to do to find out which one is prevailing in your church is to announce a change to some group's ministry and measure the reaction. There will always be a loss when things end or when a ministry that is not producing fruit is eliminated. We are not talking about that kind of normal and expected reaction. We *are* talking about hot volcanic reactions that suggest the ministry did not exist for the church at all but for the self-glorification or edification of a few at the expense of the larger mission and vision of the church in the community.

We have had to intervene in several men's studies that were meeting on church property, ordering church food, using church media, and taking advantage of church resources that had no interest in supporting the vision of our church or our pastor. Simple questions were asked to establish the connection between what they were doing and how it was benefitting both the man and the church. We found what we call "bless me" clubs inhabited by "Sponge Bobs." These are groups of men who love one another, love their gathering, love their leader, and love to soak up knowledge but have no affection or interest in producing leaders who serve the interests or initiatives of our pastor. Other characteristics include:

1. No defined goals for the man
2. No close pastoral supervision
3. No willingness to change the format to receive new believers
4. Same people
5. Stagnant or declining growth
6. Poor response to pastoral inquiry over what they are doing
7. "Talking head" teaching and knowledge focus
8. No sending, service, or missions synergy with the church or collaboration with other church ministries
9. Unwillingness to modify format for church campaigns or emphasis

They have gone rogue.

We will say it again: the Sleeping Giant process directly connects and keeps reconnecting the success of the men's ministry, its leaders, and those participating in it to the ministry traction it gives a senior or lead pastor. Courageous pastors hungry for new vitality and strength are choosing to build intentional men's ministries that reflect the character and thinking of the local church and seek to harness the men's process for that mission *as they should*. It is exciting to see men forming ranks around their pastors worldwide, pastors valuing and including their men as vital to their success, and then, together, igniting and accelerating kingdom works as one. The pride and fear in these communities of men are gone between pastors and their men. These evil-backed dynamics are being replaced with humility and faith among the leaders of the church and their men, resulting in a

> Courageous pastors hungry for new vitality and strength are choosing to build intentional men's ministries.

stronger and unified esprit de corps that transcends the stale and useless status quo of the past. Evil has a reason to be trembling at these developments in the body of Christ because unified God's men are synonymous with divine advances and manifestations of His presence.

> How good and pleasant it is when brothers live together in unity! It is like precious oil poured on the head, running down on the beard, running down on Aaron's beard, down upon the collar of his robes. It is as if the dew of Hermon were falling on Mount Zion. For there the LORD bestows his blessing, even life forevermore. (Ps. 133)

Pastors valuing and esteeming their men with value is like the taller mountain called Hermon bestowing favor and the Lord's presence on the slopes of Mount Zion below it, watering it, and the two flourish together. It is a picture of men coming together, and when they come together in covenant relationship with one another, they spark the divine hand: *"For there the LORD bestows his blessing, even life forevermore."*

Practically, our message to pastors is to work diligently on your relationship with your men. They are there to serve with you and support you in your work so that you can bear the load. Make them stakeholders in the vision, and they will make you successful. Support the development of intentional men's ministry and raise up leaders with your DNA that give you leaders to put between you and the people. On the other side, our message to the men of the church and all ministries to men in the local church is to humbly and respectfully recognize, remember, and reflect on your job: *to support your pastor and help him succeed in the mission God has given him.* He is your leader, and he is the man God has given you. Everything you do in the local church must be for the purpose of developing the man so that you can develop a leader for the mission in some form. Loyalty to your leader and recognition of his faith and sacrifice must replace any spirit of dissension and division among

> Measuring stick: Are we building a men's ministry that is purposed in every way to raise up leaders?

your ranks. The days of "bless me clubs" and Sponge Bob men's ministries that serve only themselves at the expense of advancing the health and mission of the church are over. Our continuous measuring stick must be: *Are we building a men's ministry that is purposed in every way to raise up leaders in order to make our pastor successful?* Rogue is gone.

Ranks of men standing behind their pastor stand in its place.

Key Learnings

- Rogue men's ministries operate independently whether intentionally or not and are often disconnected from the overall mission and vision of the local church.
- Disconnection from the organizational goals and developmental processes don't serve the church mission.
- There may not be evil intent, but there may be a void that good intentions desire to fill.
- Serving the greater vision will result in a healthier ministry over time.
- Developing men who guard the vision and serve others will create an explosive men's culture of Christ.
- There is no substitute for time spent in relationship and development of the men of your ministry. It must be intentional versus accidental.
- Men need to be valued and included in all aspects of the ministry in order to be a vital part of the overall church success.
- Loyalty is built through relationship and serving one another.
- Loyalty and submission to spiritual authority must replace dissention and division.

Chapter 11

Step 3: Strong Funnels That Resonate with Men

To those not having the law I became like one not having the law (though I am not free from God's law but am under Christ's law), so as to win those not having the law. To the weak I became weak, to win the weak. I have become all things to all people so that by all possible means I might save some. I do all this for the sake of the gospel, that I may share in its blessings.

1 CORINTHIANS 9:21–23

Meet *Saul Good*.

We have studied male behavior for so long now that we have made up a fictitious man named Saul Good. He is our caricature for the typical guy who's hiding issues and problems typical to men, but he is neither ready nor willing to acknowledge that these exist. When you ask him how things are going, his answer is always, "S'all good!" which is short for "It's all good." The message is: I don't need any help from anyone, I have got my life and act together, and I am sufficient within myself today. Variations on this response range from "Fine" to "Awesome" to "Great." One of the reasons for the success of the Sleeping Giant process is that you learn different hidden factors and dynamics that lie just below the surface, making the difference between success and failure with men.

This is another one of those moments. Ready?

Men are like icebergs. You only see the tip. Men love to project the image of strong, busy, purposeful, and content even when they feel weak, bored with life, and depressed. Because of their ability to compartmentalize, major issues that impact their relationships with God and people *privately* are converted to minor ones *publicly.* Thus, the response, "S'all good!" While all men practice this type of benign insincerity to some degree or another, we have found that the largest icebergs on the planet are *Christian men.* These are guys who mistakenly believe that because they have a relationship with God everything should be going much better than it really is so they don't let on. The root of this is the error in their thinking *that hardship in their life means God is absent and prosperity means He is present.* In other words, what's happening to him defines his well-being versus what's happening in him. They are professional actors and most churches that come in contact with them swallow the act. Meet Saul Good! He presents the tip of his iceberg while the jagged edges below the waterline are tearing apart the lives of those in close contact with him—including people in your body of believers. Now why start with a discussion of men and icebergs? The answer is simple but profound for our discussion.

> Men are like icebergs. You only see the tip.

You can build your ministry based on the tip or based on the reality below.

We know this will shock you, but here goes: *men lie.* Men are the masters of self-protection and self-preservation, which is both the Achilles' heel *and* the solid rocket fuel of men's ministry. Whether you are trying to attract customers to a business product or men in the congregation and community to your church, you have to ask one question before you do anything: *What are the urgent, unresolved problems people have that they need help with?* If you haven't got a handle on the answer to that question, then don't expect a lot of men to show up, keep showing up, or get other men to participate in what you are offering. One of the stinging points of the parable of the Good Samaritan was that Jesus was exposing the superficiality of the Levite and the priest who, instead of attending to the need in front of them, gave *spiritual reasons* for acting incongruently in the face of an obvious and simple need.

Let's take a look and apply it to the Sleeping Giant process with men.

> There was once a man traveling from Jerusalem to Jericho. On the way he was attacked by robbers. They took his clothes, beat him up, and went off leaving him half-dead. Luckily, a priest was on his way down the same road, but when he saw him he angled across to the other side. Then a Levite religious man showed up; he also avoided the injured man. A Samaritan traveling the road came on him. When he saw the man's condition, his heart went out to him. He gave him first aid, disinfecting and bandaging his wounds. Then he lifted him onto his donkey, led him to an inn, and made him comfortable. In the morning he took out two silver coins and gave them to the innkeeper, saying, "Take good care of him. If it costs any more, put it on my bill—I'll pay you on my way back." (Luke 10:30–35 MSG)

While most of us would never associate ourselves with the Levite or the priest in the parable, the fact is that most men's ministries in the local church are built consistently with the way the Levite and the priest *thought and responded.* That is, their ministry mentality was that men had to come to *them* on their terms versus proactively seeing and engaging men based on their big needs. Churches continue to want men to come to their existing men's structure oblivious to the real battles and needs their men are really facing. Our good intentions, good information, good events, and good music fail to enter the *real lives and needs* of men in the congregation and community. So there they lay, privately suffering and gasping for air while men's ministry in the local church walks right past them.

Huge disconnect.

After working with so many pastors and men's leaders, we have discovered the main reason their ministries tend to overlook, avoid, or miss connecting with needful men. *They would have to look at or reveal their own injuries, sin, fractures, fears, losses, or needs.* To this end, the key phrase in the parable of the Good Samaritan is: *"When he saw the man's condition, his heart went out to him."* To see another man's condition, one has to identify with that condition as a man and as a human being. To identify as a man and as a human being, we have to risk examination and exposure in our own dialogue with men. When men see or perceive us doing that, we connect. If they don't see or perceive us doing this, they disconnect.

So how is it with you?

We have trained hundreds of pastors and men's leaders in the Sleeping Giant process. Many times we have stopped our trainings or small group interactions to come alongside these leaders who are suffering themselves, but no one sees their suffering, wants to see it, or knows about it. In the process many pastors break down right in front of us as we share our own stories in the course of the training and then we ask: *"How is it with you?"* Whenever we are with men, we assume they have big needs and build our interactions with them based on that assumption versus accept the surface and enable the isolation to go on while we fill their heads full of knowledge. We are tapping into the real needs of men and modeling Step 3 of the Sleeping Giant approach in the process. We don't want our training to be just another information dump; we want them to experience God at a deeper level—a meaningful one.

> When you build your men's ministry to attract people that resemble your core leadership, you alienate the men in your congregation.

Strong funnels should attract men you don't *already have.*

When you build your men's ministry to attract people that resemble and reflect the interests and needs of your core leadership, by default you alienate the men in the congregation, in the crowd, and in the community. They are not like that group, but the irony is that churches build events and ministries to men like them! Then they don't understand why there is this huge disconnect with the other segments of men out there that they are not attracting. The final blow is when, because of their inability to see this, men's leaders label the men of their church "not committed" to make themselves feel better about the low numbers getting involved in their stuff. The church becomes the Levite and the priest in the parable, creating a men's platform that welcomes those who come to it all cleaned up and presentable versus throwing it open to the widest possible audience—men struggling outside their space who desperately want and need a victory in some area of their lives. This is the difference between other approaches and the Sleeping Giant approach: *We choose to build our ministry funnels tuned in to the needs of the man in the community, in the crowd, and in the congregation versus building ones that serve the core leadership needs.* As a result, more men actually make their way into our core leaders' from those other segments.

Meaning is everything.

Creating Magnets

"For I was hungry and you gave me something to eat, I was thirsty and you gave me something to drink, I was a stranger and you invited me in." (Matt. 25:35)

Ever ask the question: why don't men come to church-sponsored events for men? We did. Then we kept asking that question until we had thrown out just about every old way of appealing to men in order to get them connected to our life and leader development process. In the process we came face-to-face with the unpleasant reality that our "funnels" for reaching and connecting men were not strong enough. Out went the pancake breakfast funnel. Out went Monday Night Football funnel. Out went expensive and exotic men's retreats as funnels. *In* came the most unlikely but powerful funnel that changed our men's ministry. *In* came more men than

> Why don't men come to church-sponsored events for men?

we ever expected. *In* came the next generation of called leaders. *In* came waves of transformation. What funnel came in and did all that?

The pain.

We didn't just stumble onto this powerful vehicle for reaching men; it was there the whole time in our own lives and in the lives of men all around us. We read the research, we did our homework like many of you, and we made attempts to deal with pressing men's issues with special groups or classes. What we had not done is build a platform that made the core pains of men the starting point *for every man in our church* to begin the life and leader development journey with us. We had plenty of men, which meant we also had plenty of real needs living and breathing below the waterlines of their lives to trigger a response for help. We reasoned that this mother lode of pain was sitting there like an untapped vein of gold lying just beneath our feet. But were we right? More daunting: How could we build a funnel large enough to find out?

Answer: *Father's Day.*

We approached our pastor and asked if we could have some of our guys give their testimony as a *part of his message to the men.* Each of these men would give his testimony and talk about how their men's group was helping them to face, confront, and get a "win" in a certain area on an increasing basis. Each man would speak to an uncomfortable area below the waterline but shine the light on himself, giving men permission to admit having the same struggle. At the end of each testimony, the speaker would say, "If you are like me and are struggling with—being a good father, overcoming temptation, being a good husband, or connecting with strong Christian men . . . then check the card in your bulletin and join us this week."

> Hungry, Feed: Naked, Clothed

> We had plenty of men, which meant we also had plenty of real needs living below the waterlines of their lives.

Our pastor gave an awesome message to men and after every point said, "Now I would like you to hear from Chris, Russ, Phil," and so on. Our men had never been so meaningfully addressed within a service before. You could feel the waterline on every man's iceberg coming down, the level of reality rising, and the liberating presence of freedom to do something about it in every service. The men were told if they wanted to get into the same process these men did and start getting healthy, all they needed to do was check a simple response card and put it in the offering plate. But would they do it?

Through the funnel of *real felt needs,* 895 icebergs fell into our laps.

We called it HERD "U" as in Herd University. It was a place where all the men of our church would start their journey into character and Christlikeness as well as begin the leadership development pathway. They would come because they had a real issue that was affecting their ability to love God, people, or both. They would come because the pain of the problem exceeded the fear of change connected to the problem. They would come because they didn't want to lose their marriage. They would come because they were tired of moral and spiritual compromise that made them feel like boys and not men. They would come because they were desperate to connect with other men of God heading in the same direction. They would come because they needed a "win," and men in our church were giving their testimonies of victories through connecting into men's community. They would come and keep coming because the tools were good, the relationships were strong, and a larger leadership vision was cast for them beyond the resolution of their problems.

> They would come because they had a real issue that was affecting their ability to love God, people, or both.

It was a stunning and surprisingly welcomed confirmation of the Sleeping Giant premise, but it wasn't because we created anything or appealed to their intellect. We simply called out what was *already present and inside them waiting to come out.* That is how strong funnels and magnets for men are created within a church culture. You ask, *What*

urgent and unresolved problems are men facing and needing help with?
Then you build platforms, testimonies, bridges, and multiple opportunities for them to say yes to winning transformation of that area. The men who come in through the funnels of pain and felt needs to what we call the "GET IN and GET HEALTHY" platform are leaders in process. We assume this because something inside these guys is compelling them to be God's men or be better men. That spark is divine—a divine calling to a transcendent purpose that he only dimly sees through the lens of his need now *but* will soon morph beyond self-preservation to his purpose and calling.

It is the Holy Spirit.

One assumption that the Sleeping Giant process makes is that the Holy Spirit is not failing in the lives of men regarding sin, righteousness, and judgment. He is actively working in the lives of men, diligently collaborating with their conscience, and forcefully speaking through consequences and circumstances to draw men to God. He wants to transform these men who are hungry for freedom, purpose, victory, influence, leadership, significance, and meaning into God's men who go from the ranks of the audience to the army. But for that to happen, both the call and the funnels for them to join the Spirit's process have to be direct, strong, intentional, and prophetic in both the truth telling and mystical senses of the ministry. When it is done right, the call is authentic and transparent, accepting and affirming, and filled with the authority and accountability of God. You can't dance.

When God calls, a man doesn't dance—he comes.

> Pain acts like a window cleaner in a man's life: what was once foggy or unclear before is now, because of the pain, crystal clear.

The Holy Spirit is not just calling men who are in the hurt lockers of life. However, we have learned that pain acts like window cleaner in a man's life: *what was once foggy or unclear before is now, because of the pain, crystal clear.* Pain is also a powerful motivator because all men want relief from it and are eager to engage solutions that will help with that process. We have also learned that when you build funnels around the core felt needs in men's lives, you discover other types of pain that work just as well as the pains connected to relational or moral failures. These magnets for men act as strong funnels because of their private need and personal hardwiring by God.

STRONG FUNNELS THAT RESONATE WITH MEN				
Pain	Purpose	People	Power	Play
Marriage	Cause	Fraternity	Influence	Fun
Family	Battle	Team	Significance	Laughter
Character	Loyalty	Accountability	Greatness	Pleasure
Temptation	Transcendence	Acceptance	Leadership	Risk
Isolation	Justice	Affirmation	Position	Adventure

While the pain resonator is how a lot of men find their way into men's community, large numbers come in through the absence of purpose, people, power, or play in their lives. Men want a cause, want a team, want to achieve, and want the *feeling* connected to positive results in those areas of their lives. This is why the journey must include a vision that goes beyond getting healthy relationally and spiritually. There has to be a reason for getting healthy, and that reason is this: *to leave a footprint for God on earth.* All events, activities, topics, teaching, tools, and processes must drip with these themes in order to resonate practically and powerfully with men.

"No Pole Vaulting"

"Go to Class 101."

The year was 1989, and those words flowed out of Rick Warren's mouth in response to an ambitious young missionary who had just asked him the following question: "What do you have for leaders?" I remember feeling pretty stupid afterward for assuming that I was a leader and asking the pastor if I could jump right into his leadership community as an unknown guy and new attender. So after picking my ego up off the floor, exiting the room, and returning to church the following weekend, I signed my wife and myself up for "Class 101: Membership." I remember telling my wife that it was fours long but that our pastor was directing me to do this and that we needed to do it.

My pastor was simply being intentional.

That four-hour session was taught by Pastor Rick himself. We heard his story of how he showed up in the Saddleback Valley with a U-Haul trailer, his new wife, two hundred dollars, and a vision for a church that would one day welcome twenty-five thousand members. We saw his heart, felt his faith, and experienced the presence of the Holy Spirit calling us to enter this amazing adventure. He downloaded his vision for a healing community of broken people doing life together and becoming like Christ. He pondered openly about our congregation being the one that would move beyond the walls of the church into the community to meet real needs and minister. He loaded us onto his ship and transported us to the world, unashamedly declaring that this church would be dedicated to seeing people reached for Christ locally and globally. And then, true to his word, he invited those present who did not have a relationship with Christ to take a step, cross the line of commitment, and invite Him to be their leader and Lord.

> He implanted his DNA in us that day.

He implanted his DNA in us that day.

We like sharing that story with churches we train because when you build strong funnels for men, there can be no pole vaulting over that process of beginning the journey. Rick listened to me, heard me explain that I was a missionary, had been to seminary, and was qualified experientially. But he also knew that none of those things would help him unless I had his vision and mission planted firmly inside of me. Classes 101 through 401 were there for a specific reason: to ensure that anybody serving in leadership understood the heart of the church.

"Go to Class 101."

In hindsight all I have to say is: brilliant! What a comfort it must have been to Rick to know that he had a safe and strong funnel whereby people could enter a life and leader development process that would ensure that the right DNA and disciplines would be trained into his people. I never forgot that experience; and later on, when setting up the process for men at Saddleback, I, too, wanted the comfort and assurance of a strong funnel that downloaded the DNA of the vision and mission of men's ministry within our church. I can't tell you how many times I have said to men of all backgrounds and levels of maturity who want to get involved in men's ministry, "Go to our GET IN and GET HEALTHY classes and then we'll talk." It's there that I know they will:

> Building strong funnels is ensuring that the culture is consistent, strong, and deeply imbedded into each man entering the process.

- Explore the core issues men are dealing with.
- Dive into God's Word.
- Practice biblical openness and confession with other men.
- Transform through fellowship and accountability.
- Be connected with one of my leaders.
- Hear the vision of leadership we have for them.
- Begin to be followed relationally through the process.

Building strong funnels is more than just resonating with the souls of men; it is ensuring that the culture is consistent, strong, and deeply imbedded into each man entering the process. These funnels connected to the felt needs of men also become centers of transformation in men's lives which produce strong advocates and ambassadors drawing the net even wider. All prefunnel events that men encounter draw them into this one starting-point funnel in one way, shape, or form including:

- Men inquiring from the Web
- Men inquiring at the weekend services
- Men attending catalytic events
- Men connecting through special emphases like Father's Day

- Men talking with my leaders
- Participating men who are transforming and recruiting other men
- Men in deep pain who come to the church office for lay counseling
- Women's ministry directing wives to tell their husbands

Step 3 of the Sleeping Giant process is crucial both from a content and a structural perspective. Key thoughts include:

1. Your funnels or entry points have to meet real needs.
2. Those needs have to be regularly addressed, highlighted, and messaged in all you do.
3. Your tools have to fit the felt needs of men who are coming.
4. The leaders sitting in this zone of entry have to shepherd and care diligently for all the men who fall into the process.
5. Once your funnels have been identified, selected, and outfitted with tools and people, there is only one thing left to do—fill them up!

Doing this for churches has been both the result and the thrill of doing Every Man conferences worldwide. Intentionally connecting men into groups through a strong funnel and watching those men enter a life and leader development process for sponsoring churches is *the* outcome we want. The Sleeping Giant approach always brings this one result: *men connected to an ongoing process that promotes the vision of the church, meets the needs of the man, and develops a leader to deploy.* (For information on scheduling a funnel event for your church, go to www.everymanministries.com.)

> Men connected to an ongoing process that promotes the vision of the church, meets the needs of the man, and develops a leader to deploy.

The key to building strong funnels that load men into your life and leader development process is recognizing the unresolved problems men are dealing with, seeing past the outward tips of men's lives, and regularly and publicly addressing the realities of the battles they are facing to create a continuous flow that looks like this.

1. Funnel event that helps a man say yes to connection.
2. Connect the man to a group of other men in his area of need.
3. Engage and encourage him in the group process.
4. Cast vision for his next steps.
5. Plan more funnel events.
6. Back to Step 1.

You can feel that with the progression and execution of each step the Sleeping Giant process is intended to feel tight, connected, and simple. We move from strong vision and mission to a strong pastoral alignment to strong funnels that resonate with the souls of men. The next step in the Sleeping Giant process considers the question every man who comes into the funnel of your ministry is automatically asking whether he is verbalizing it or not.

"Now that you got me, what are you going to do with me?"

Time to move to Step 4.

Key Learnings

- Taking the relational time to ask the next questions and listening to men will uncover what lies beneath the inculturated surface of a man.
- One must discover the underlying unresolved issues for your culture of men in order to capture the heart of a man.
- The real lives of men will initially attract them to the ministry born out of their need. In this case his pain will win over head knowledge initially.
- Do you model the same needs and issues in your own life and show how God is directing you?
- The uncommitted men in your church may be a direct reflection of your leadership.

- Men need places they perceive to be safe to admit their struggles and the freedom it brings to be able to do something about them.
- Your process for bringing a man into community where he can be healed must connect to and facilitate deep discipleship.
- The spark has already been placed within men through the Holy Spirit and our challenge is to ignite it.
- The payoff for a man to "Get In" must be obvious and simple in order to move him to the next step and to understand the developmental journey that lies ahead for him.
- Real needs in the lives of men must be addressed to gain a beachhead in the process that connects him to the mission and vision of the church.

Chapter 12

Step 4: Strong Spiritual Pathway

*The path of the righteous is like the first gleam of dawn,
shining ever brighter till the full light of day.*

PROVERBS 4:18

My engine stalled.

There was no warning. I was traveling at seventy miles per hour, one mile from my exit, and eager to get home from a four-day trip when it happened. No dashboard indicators came on, no sounds came from the engine, and I had plenty of gas. In a split second I went from all good to all bad. I went from full power to no power. I went from a positive anticipation of getting home to a boiling frustration over getting stuck. All of my physical and emotional momentum ran into a wall, and in a loud, mad, sardonic explosion of consternation I shouted: "Really!" As in, "Hey God, I am just trying to get home to my family. I am hot, I stink, I am supertired, superhungry, and superdepleted. Now this? Really!" The vision of a relaxing afternoon in shorts and a T-shirt, sipping a cool drink, and watching my game vaporized. I was stuck on the side of the road and would remain there for a while. I screamed. Then I repented. Then I prayed. Then I accepted it as just life. But don't be fooled; it didn't make what happened *any less frustrating.* No man likes

> Just keep in
> mind that
> word—
> *frustration.*

being thwarted when he feels he is close to his goal or is headed in the right direction. So what do stalled engines, thwarted aspirations, and major frustration have to do with Step 4 of the Sleeping Giant process? Strangely— *everything* and, hopefully, nothing *in the future*.

Just keep in mind that word—*frustration.*

Inspiration without Progression

Chris rose out of his seat and walked onto the stadium field.

For the last forty-five minutes it was as if the speaker had been handed a personal file on Chris's life, and then he proceeded to publicly unravel his life story as thirty thousand men listened in. Each story, each Bible verse, each insight, and each observation resonated deeply; and Chris could feel something funny inside—it was like he was going to give birth. God was clearly extending Himself in a supernatural way to Chris, speaking to him personally, and calling him to a new life. Then the speaker shifted his focus to Chris and thousands of men just like him when he said, "God was calling to Himself tonight." The music began to play, and the speaker invited all those men who felt God spoke to them tonight to "get up out of your seats right now, make your way forward to the stadium field, and say yes to God with your feet." Within ten seconds Chris was at the gate leading to the stadium field in what seemed like an ocean of men pouring out of the stands, onto the grass, and toward the stage. He had never been so inspired, so hopeful, or so personally convinced that this decision to become a Christian would be the best decision of his life.

Four years later Chris recounted this story for me but not with the affection and appreciation one might expect. The grateful attitudes were absent, and in their place were deep frustration and irritation after finally finding what had been missing for the last four years—connection to other men in a church with a clear vision, deep relationships, and intentional progression of development. "If only I had found you guys four years ago," he said. I was wincing as he talked because I totally identified with Chris's story from both sides. Many times I had been the "speaker" in his story watching God's Spirit engulf and consume men, bringing them sincerely and humbly to His throne of salvation through Christ. No words can describe the power of the gospel in those moments. Unfortunately I also knew exactly what he was talking about when he began to recount the pattern of the weeks, months, and years following that night of inspiration. His story played like a broken record that kept repeating itself for hundreds of thousands of men who never successfully "reentered" their local houses of worship in the context of men. They had to reenter them in the context of women and kids in the absence of any strong vision or programming for the men. I would be frustrated and irritated too.

Meet the "Rocket Booster Boys."

These are men who, after being inspired spiritually, motivated personally, and activated emotionally, eventually plummet to earth as the fuel of their initial salvation or reignition as God's man wears off. These men believe they have escaped the atmosphere of low-level living, low-level character, and low-level significance for something transcendent only to be *thwarted* in their journey by an unexpected engine stall they didn't see coming. Their stories include many if not all of the following characteristics.

1. Strong decision for Christ.
2. Enthusiastic start and positive outlook on his spiritual life.
3. High motivation to change and learn: "I was on fire."
4. A search for a church with men's ministry.
5. Participation in a few men's events that did not resonate.
6. No regular connection to other men for the purpose of spiritual growth.
7. Normal pressures over time.
8. Old ways of dealing with pressure take over again.
9. Attending but not activated within the church.
10. Decreased passion for things of God.
11. Resumption of the life he was living before but now as a believer.
12. Frustration and confusion over why his church doesn't have a men's vision and pathway.

With few exceptions Chris told of a similar journey. My inward and outward reaction to Chris was the same as it was to the numerous men who told me similar stories before him. I said, "I am so sorry," followed by, "That should never be." I wince in pain, and then I frown in anger over the four lost years. I hurt for the man, and I get mad at the church for orphaning men like Chris who had to wait an entire year before feeling the strength and power again that he experienced that first night. I wonder how many I led to Christ from those platforms who, like Chris, felt so much promise at the start, only to have the joy of their salvation grow stale and distant because the church had no landing zones or process ready to receive these newborn boys. I reflected on how men's ministry in the local church was reproducing the same cycle of frustration in men who, after great inspiration, made little progression after searching earnestly for a safe and strong place *in their own church* where men are developed spiritually and intentionally *as men*. This is why Step 4 of the Sleeping Giant process is the most important step in the process and the one step upon which the success of your efforts hinge.

You must have a *strong spiritual pathway for men.*

The math of Chris's story is simple: *inspiration without progression leads to confusion and frustration.* Many churches are good at gathering men, and many parachurch ministries are good at gathering men for churches. *Few* are good at keeping them connected and bringing them on a meaningful journey into personal character and leadership. That's frustrating for the man and for the church, each of whom anticipated so much more coming out of their efforts. More poignantly, it is poor stewardship of God's money and resources if the man is "orphaned" after the event by the process. Once a man comes into your men's ministry through a strong funnel, has risked coming to an event or connecting with other guys at church, you must proactively address the natural questions floating around in the back of his head that sound like this:

> A strong pathway is the core process you hang your entire men's ministry on.

- "Now that you have me, what are you going to do with me?"
- "What's the process?"
- "Is this it?"
- "Where do I fit in this place?"
- "How do they view my presence and participation?"
- "How long before I connect again?"
- "What's the plan?"
- "What is my next step?"

A strong pathway is the core process you hang your entire men's ministry on. If you don't have one, you need one. If you do have one, it better be rock solid and resonate to men. The purpose of step four of the Sleeping Giant process eliminates inspiration without progression that leads to frustration, disappointment, and disconnection. Take a look at the following progression. It shows the dynamics of a strong connective funnel experience and the intentional linking of that event to a solid pathway to continue the journey and avoid *spiritual engine stalls.*

The Missing "Linkage"		
Provide a Strong Funnel in Order to:		**Point to and Provide a Strong Pathway in Order to:**
Gain Connection	**Intentionally and**	Continue Connection
Tap Motivation	**Proactively**	Build On Motivation
Provide Inspiration	**Address Questions**	Cast Vision
Produce Activation	**Men Are Asking In Their Minds**	Divine Calling
Begin Transformation		Strong Progression
New or Unactivated Believer		Deployed Leader

> He wasn't seeing it in the local church so he went back to the one place that seemed to understand his needs . . . the world.

Now back to our man Chris—*the actual user and feedback provider*. After Chris walked onto the field and gave his life to Christ, he was searching for a continued connection and strong pathway to build on his motivation to be God's man in the local church *where he lives*. The funnel was gone, and the pathway was needed to continue the journey. But he searched in vain to find a strong pathway and people to match the strength of his of his initial launch. He did find a hodgepodge of special interest and special knowledge Bible studies, annual events, and lots of books for men, but there was no framework or larger vision into which all of them fit. He couldn't see a clear beginning, middle, and end with intentions and goals. Chris is not unlike most men—he loves clarity and intentionality if he is going to invest his time and energy. He wasn't seeing it in the local church so he went back to the one place that seemed to understand his need for some clarity, excellence, structure, vision, and purpose—the world.

His engine stalled.

Four years later he ran head-on into the Sleeping Giant model, and his journey was reignited. Chris has brought numerous men through the process himself and is living the adventure every man of God *believes he will experience* when he comes to Christ. He is not frustrated anymore; he is activated. He's not in the audience passively attending church; he's in the army aggressively serving and sharing. He's not isolated; he is connected. He is not retreating backward into the world; he is risking for the kingdom and moving forward. And since there are millions upon millions of Chris's in every country and culture waiting to be reignited by the local church, it is time to enter the most impactful part of our discussion.

The adoption of a strong spiritual pathway for men in local churches worldwide.

First, we will show you a visual diagram of the model we have built and tested over the last ten years. It *really* helps to see it versus just explain it. **Second,** we will define the core goals the Sleeping Giant model accomplishes for the man and for the church. **Third,** we will describe what occurs at each phase of the process. **Fourth,** we will show you how the Sleeping Giant pathway achieves the core spiritual formation goals called for in Scripture. As we walk through this discussion, we know a few things are going to happen:

1. You will see or recognize what is missing in your men's ministry or process. That can be some or all of the pieces.
2. You will see or recognize you have certain pieces of the pathway that exist already. This is good. In this case your mission will be to place them in the right location.
3. You will see or recognize language that is close to your own churches values. Feel free to go ahead and substitute your church's language for ours.
4. You will have lots of questions! Write them down and if, by the end of the book and assessment process, we have not answered them, just e-mail us.

Saddleback Men's Pathway

THE MEN'S PATHWAY

BE GOD'S MAN

BE A SERVANT   BE LOYAL   BE A BROTHER

BE A MESSENGER

The "Be" DNA of our Church

If you have read or are familiar with *The Purpose Driven Church* or *The Purpose Driven Life*, then you know that our church values and vision revolve around realizing five core purposes in the lives of believers. They are:

1. Worship . . . to love God and please Him in all thoughts and actions
2. Fellowship . . . to be connected to a spiritual family on a consistent basis
3. Discipleship . . . to become like Christ in our character
4. Ministry . . . to use your God-given SHAPE to serve the body of Christ
5. Mission . . . to make disciples by sharing the gospel personally, locally, and globally

The first thing we tell churches when it comes time to build a strong pathway is this: your core process MUST reflect the DNA and values of *your church.* What you see is our attempt to integrate the values of our pastor and our church into our pathway. Those values are reflected in all of the "be" statements residing in the diagram. The first thing you will notice is that the actual words in our core values are missing! In their place are character qualities that reflect each of those values *in a man's life.* Early on in this process I remember telling my pastor, "Rick, the purposes are for everyone, *but they are lived out in the context of our gender as men and women.* Worship for me means something different in practice than it does for my wife. Fellowship looks different for me than it does for wife. My issues of growth and discipleship are different from hers. And so is the way we approach service and missions." He replied, "That's good, Kenny, I have to write that down. Say that again." To this end, in the model you see our core values reframed so that they resonate *for a man.* Here's how they match up along with their scriptural foundations.

> The church's core process MUST reflect the DNA and values of your church.

1. Worship is *be loyal*. A man is always loyal to who he loves. (John 15:13)
2. Fellowship is *be a brother*. A man craves and needs brotherhood and fraternity. (2 Tim. 2:22)
3. Discipleship is *be God's man*. A man's identity determines his energy and expression. Discipleship is becoming like Christ. (Rom. 8:29, 2 Cor. 3:18)
4. Ministry is *be a servant*. A man's true strength is his ability to say no to himself to say yes to others. (Matt. 20:28)
5. Mission is *be a messenger*. A man talks to others about that which excites him most and has had the most impact on him. Whether he is excited about cars or Christ, men are messengers of what they like or love. (Matt. 28:18–20)

This reframing accomplished several things. **First,** it shows that men's ministry is aligned with the vision and values of our church. **Second,** it creates a language that resonates with men *and* supports the purposes in their lives. **Third,** it takes the value from a concept and turns it into a character quality we want the man to develop. **Fourth,** there is consistency and familiarity in our communication to the men of the congregation. **Fifth,** the five "be" transformations represent tangible inner works produced by a *living faith*. As a man journeys through our pathway we are going to see him transform and change from the *inside out*. Now the question is: What steps does the man take to see those transformations come to pass?

Glad you asked!

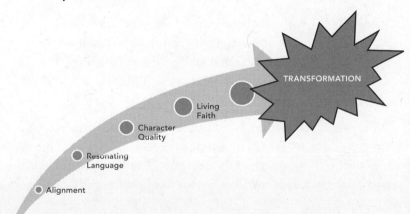

What Do I Do?

"Just tell me what I need *to do*."

Men are *doers,* which is both a strength and a weakness. Since we are the "point and shoot" gender for the most part, the mistake churches make with men's ministry is that they go about in the wrong order. As in, *ready . . . FIRE! . . . aim.* They get men all fired up for God but fail to have a plan or process to capture and direct all that firepower for the good of the church. The Sleeping Giant model is a proven remedy for the trigger-happy methodology of unintentional men's ministry. It realigns the process for churches to hit the target: *Ready . . . AIM . . . fire!* It's good to want your men to be excited for Christ and transform. It's better to have a simple action plan that tells him *what to do* in order for those goals to be realized. It's best to have them working together. Like we tell all the churches we train: *good is always the enemy of the best.*

> "Ready . . . AIM . . . fire!" must replace "Ready . . . FIRE! . . . then aim."

"*Ready . . . AIM . . . fire!*" must replace "*Ready . . . FIRE! . . . then aim.*"

That's what you see in the model. That's why you see the "be" goals (of core purpose transformations) and the "do" actions required for those goals to be achieved together. Those actions are reflected in the phrases:

1. **Get IN** . . . with other men who share your convictions.
2. **Get HEALTHY** . . . relationally and morally as a man.
3. **Get STRONG** . . . biblically and spiritually as a disciple.
4. **Get GOING** . . . into your personal leadership expressions of ministry and mission.

When we talk about our men's pathway, these four simple concepts explain everything we are about, what the process is, and what the endgame is with guys who want to participate. The best thing about the Sleeping Giant model is this: *not a lot of explanation is required.* Men understand these concepts without thinking! But for your sake here's the idea behind each action step along the pathway.

"Get In"

Every man's "gotta guy" they know who can help you fix your car, write your next home loan, or help you manage your money. But most men don't "gotta guy" that helps them win battles for spiritual and relational health. Our model emphasizes getting guys "IN" with other guys who share a personal commitment to grow personally and spiritually. That could be a weekly men's group. It could be the men in your couples group meeting on a separate day of the week. It could be some guys from work having coffee once a week. It could be a meeting of men at church or at a conference that connects you to other men who seek God's purposes for their lives and relationships. When a man commits to pursuing and deepening his male friendships, he will sustain his momentum and achieve personal changes faster than he ever could by himself.

> Men need to "get in" every day, at every event, in every class, and in every place where men gather until it is coming out of their eyeballs.

Men become men in the company of other men. Ask any warrior in any culture. And for God's man, who wants to do life God's way, connecting with other men is not optional. We tell men they need to "get in" every day, at every event, in every class, and in every place where men gather until it is coming out of their eyeballs. Why so much energy?

It starts his journey from inspiration to progression.

Action step one of the Sleeping Giant spiritual pathway is *always* "get into" a strong men's community in the local church. This will look different depending on the structure of your church. In our church we encourage men who are married to join a couples small group because we know that in a couples group they will find men to do life with as well as a larger life group of families. We want a man in community with other men who know his wife and family so that when he connects with the guys there is tribal knowledge of his relationships and issues (we will talk in more detail about this strategy in chapter 14). Other men start with a large-group Bible study, and this becomes the avenue for small group connection within a large-group setting. Other men come straight to a "Get Healthy" class based on a need they have which compels them to connect out of the pain. After just a few questions, we can determine what the best setting is for a man to make a connection with other men that will be the most meaningful. In a men's culture that values connection, men who come into your church will see, feel, hear about, and be asked if they are connected to a good men's group. The goal is that the "GET IN" value is modeled, messaged by your men, and mentored into the DNA of the guys who connect with your ministry as central to the life and depth of the men's community.

Our next call after "GET IN" provides direction and meaning once guys get connected. They will naturally want to know: "OK, I am in. What now?"

Time for "do" step number two.

"Get Healthy"

Step two of the process involves defining and meeting the felt needs of men and helping them get a "win" that is meaningful to *them*.

We have talked about the fact that men are like icebergs in the sense that they only reveal the *tip* of who they are and what is happening in their lives. But underneath the waterline of their lives are a host of issues that are producing enormous stress and pressure morally, relationally, maritally, professionally, and emotionally that define the true substance of their existence. There's a word for this type of iceberg existence: *acting!* Again, Step 2 of the process involves defining and meeting the felt needs of men and helping them get a "win" that is meaningful to *them*.

The basis of having a "Get Healthy" phase of your pathway is this: *if the most real and relevant issues remain unaddressed and untouched, the rest of what a man may learn or accomplish through his connection with other men will be short-lived in both the life and church contexts.* He will simply become a more knowledgeable roadside bomb waiting to go off later in the leader development process because of unaddressed character issues. The guy implodes on your watch, you never knew anything was going on, and you didn't care enough to find out if he was healthy *first*.

Ouch.

In a group context and with group safety, men need to go after core health in their own character and relationships *first*. This involves an open discussion of temptation and compromise *(moral health)*, his view of women and marriage *(marital health)*, his leadership in the home *(family health)*, and how masculine friendship and accountability work *(relational health)*. True health in these core areas is the difference between an authentic versus a synthetic leader. More important, the Bible requires core health and strong leadership in these categories *prior* to selection for church leadership (1 Tim. 3:1–5).

To see the GET HEALTHY tools and resources connected to the Sleeping Giant pathway for men, scan this QR code with your mobile device or go to lifeway.com/kennyluck.

No Health Step   vs.   with A Health Step

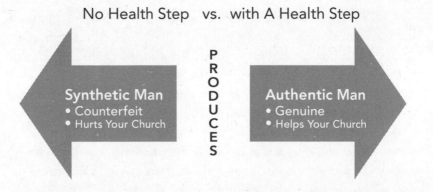

P
R
O
D
U
C
E
S

Synthetic Man
• Counterfeit
• Hurts Your Church

Authentic Man
• Genuine
• Helps Your Church

Get In and **Get Healthy** are powerfully connected parts of the pathway *for the man and for the church*. Here's why and how they work together.

1. Men who transform together tend to stay together and finish the process together. They have gone to war on major issues in their

lives and celebrated major victories in those same areas. They have bonded deeply.

2. A church that sponsors transformation of men helps itself by winning the loyalty, energy, and expression of its men toward the larger needs, mission, and vision of the church. The transformed man is naturally asking: "What's next?" and "How can I give back?" We call this *transformational capital* that gets put into the bank account of the church. Withdrawals can be made from this powerful account at a later time and allocated toward important church initiatives. Pastors need to understand an important Sleeping Giant principle: *transformed men are like money in the bank!*

Once a church has defined and met the felt needs of a man, the transformational capital earned by the church in that man's life needs to be spent on leadership development and spiritual training.

Time for "do" step number three.

"Get Strong"

With a solid baseline of health intact, a vision for his continued involvement must be cast and a process of discipleship must be in place that prepares him for deployment into his ministry within the church and into his mission in the world. This next call will involve a higher stake in the vision of the church, a higher commitment, and a higher cost. The **Get Strong** educational and experiential phase of the pathway is about making a man of God.

In an established relational context, the focus here is exploring and experiencing the core beliefs and behaviors of God's man. It is the natural progression from transformation to activation to leadership training. Practically, men will feel themselves going to the next level of commitment personally, spiritually, and practically in ministry. In this phase they are packing on serious spiritual muscle and disciplines as well as engaging resources and relationships that center on strong spiritual formation. The goal? A strong and aggressive spiritual expression of the Great Commandment and the Great Commission evidenced in his life. This is reflected in his commitment to:

1. **Christlikeness** . . . A man of God committed to God's **DREAM** for personal transformation in his life on a daily basis
2. **Conquering by faith** . . . A man of God who will consistently **RISK** in the direction of God's purposes and promises to advance the kingdom
3. **Confronting evil** . . . A man of God who understands how to **FIGHT** evil within himself and in all domains of his life.
4. **Cooperating with the Holy Spirit** . . . A man of God who **SOARS** by rising above cultural masculinity through a Spirit-filled and formed life.

Once fully trained in these ways, there is only one call left for a strong man. Time for "do" step number four.

"Get Going"

The bird must leave the nest, start flapping, and start flying into his purpose.

The first steps in the process defined and met the core needs of men in the community and congregation (**Get In and Get Healthy**). The next phase captured the motivation created by transformations in men's lives with a forceful vision and call to spiritual growth (**Get Strong**). The last and most natural transition is to deploy these men to serve the church and aggressively share the gospel in all ways within their life context (**Get Going**). In the Sleeping Giant model a trained "God's man" should be responsible for ministry, reproducing leaders, and replacing pastoral staff in the execution and delivery of ministry to the people. The message to the man coming from the process is: *we want you at your post and need you at your post to succeed.*

To see the GET STRONG tools and resources connected to the Sleeping Giant pathway for men, scan this QR code with your mobile device or go to lifeway.com/kennyluck.

We intentionally don't engineer this phase like the others because both ministry and mission expressions are numerous and person-specific according to their gifts and callings. The fact is that churches typically *don't lack* ministry or mission opportunities for their people, *but they do lack the men and muscle* to drive them!

"Get Going" is the call to get off their "blessed assurance" and get into the adventure of advancing in the kingdom.

Bringing It All Together for Spiritual Formation

This next visual shows you why both the "be" and the "do" elements of a strong spiritual pathway are needed in order to make a healthy disciple who lives the authentic Christian life. The Bible advises us strongly that we do our spiritual math.

The Math of Spiritual Formation

Living Faith (BE)—Living Works (DO) = Dead Faith

Living Works (DO)—Living Faith (BE) = Dead Works

Living Faith (BE) + Living Works (DO) = Authentic Christian Life

---

In the Sleeping Giant model a trained "God's man" should be responsible for ministry, reproducing leaders, and replacing pastoral staff.

If a man under my care claims to have great faith and a close relationship but there are no real changes in his behaviors or life, the Bible calls that a dead faith and exposes his claim as not God at all. This man is the one who loves to talk about the Bible and is quick to give his unvarnished opinions on all things God but doesn't want to connect with other men on a consistent basis, serve in a ministry, or witness God's love to his neighbor (BE – DO = Dead Faith). If that same man is doing a ton of ministry for God but is consistently abusing and mistreating his wife, has huge anger issues, and does not feel the need to change, the Bible calls his actions for God dead works (DO – BE = Dead Works). Both of these profiles of men are spiritually dysfunctional and will invite God's discipline. However, when a man is inwardly changing in his character and that change inwardly is manifesting in new actions that show love for God and people, that is a true God's man (BE + DO = Living Faith + Living Works). The reason we share this is because many churches and men's

> We want men to move meaningfully from a place of inspiration to solid progression.

ministry models are weighted heavily toward one side or the other. One church is high spiritual awareness and development but is low on spiritual actions. The other is low on spiritual awareness and development but heavy on spiritual works. One claims character change is king. The other claims conduct is king.

The Bible clearly says *you need both* operating.

Now you have seen and know why our spiritual pathway is built the way it is. We want it to produce authentic leaders versus synthetic actors! We want men to move meaningfully from a place of inspiration to solid progression. We want all churches in the body of Christ to possess standing armies of men whose lives reflect the integrity, character, and truth of a truly biblical and relational process. We hope you share that desire with us and will join the movement of churches putting the Sleeping Giant model to work for the men in your church. We will be talking about the tools and people you will need at each step in the chapters to come, but for now we trust we have you thinking about how your church can start meaningfully helping men by showing them how to:

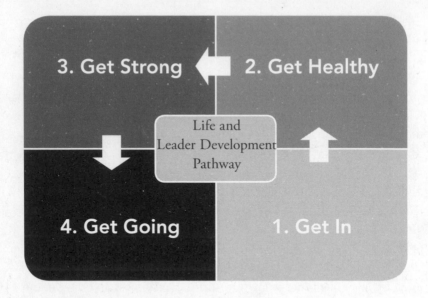

The goal: No more stalled engines!

Key Learnings

- Inspiration is not enough for those on a new journey, a follow-up place for him to land is critical to engaging the man.
- Men need a safe place to be welcomed and developed spiritually.
- Intentional funnel events and experiences need to link to a solid process for the development of a man.
- If the local church does not provide developmental zones, culture will.
- The larger vision must contain a spiritual development pathway leading to activation not just head knowledge.
- The developmental pathway must be consistent with the culture or DNA of your church.
- Ultimately one must be concerned with the life transformation of each man; this is one of the measures of success.
- BE—Becoming more and more like Christ, living faith.
- DO—Producing living works out of Christlikeness.

- GET IN—Connecting with other guys who share a commitment to grow.
- GET HEALTHY—Identifying and meeting felt needs to triage a man to health.
- GET STRONG—A higher commitment to be deeply discipled.
- GET GOING—Reaching out to others, reproducing and training the next leaders.

Chapter 13

Step 5: Strong Relational Core

Jonathan said to David, "Go in peace, for we have sworn friendship with each other in the name of the LORD saying, 'The LORD is witness between you and me, and between your descendants and my descendants forever.'"

1 SAMUEL 20:42

"Mind the gap."

I will never forget hearing these words for the first time as a visitor to the UK. In the London underground, as the train pulls into the station and just before the doors open to let people on and off, you will hear a voice from above say, *"Mind the gap."* I quizzed my fellow Brits and came to learn that the phrase was introduced in the late sixties to warn passengers to take caution while crossing "the gap" between the train door and the station platform. Depending on the platform this gap can be wide or narrow, but they all present potential danger. If you are not *minding the gap*, you might be *stepping into the gap* and *bridging the gap* from life to death prematurely! I get it now.

Friendly voice. Specific reminder. Successful passage.

This message of paying attention to something specific *mid-process* so you can successfully arrive at your destination is exactly the picture of where we are in the Sleeping Giant process. Just as riders of the "tubes"

> A strong spiritual pathway gives cohesion, but a strong relational infrastructure drives everything forward.

in London might brush off the admonition to "mind the gap" out of habit, there is a habit churches seem to have that is subtle, and it's this: trusting tools, strategy, program, and process while, at the same time, *forgetting to foster the deep relationships needed to make strong community a reality.* The cart of program and tactics is placed before the horse of relationships. The key concept is this: *A strong spiritual pathway gives cohesion, but a strong relational infrastructure drives everything forward.* Possessing a heart to reach men is good, but without healthy personal accounts full of relational capital throughout your ranks, no amount of heart can win success. Listen up: the quality of the relationships among the men in your ministry *is the gap* between success and failure. And as we leave the platform of strategy to advance into the area of implementation, we want to be that friendly voice which offers you a specific reminder that will help ensure you achieve your goals.

Mind the gap.

Just as people in a hurry fail to mind the gap closely because their mind is focused on other things, churches fail to mind the gap of relational depth within their men's ministry because they have other priorities on their minds. Those priorities of the ministry take precedence over cultivating strong personal bonds and connections, steal the lion's share of energy, and divert attention over to things like committees, events, meetings, and projects. After seeing and experiencing these types of men's cultures we have discovered that there is an uncomfortable reason for this style—the other priorities make less emotional and physical demands than real relationship building. In other words, relationships are messy, and the prospect of that scares us away from entering the lives of men in an authentic way. So seemingly by default but really by intention, the men's leadership team emphasizes anything other than one-on-one relationship building because—awkward pause—it's easier!

What do we mean?

It's easier to answer Bible questions than to answer personal questions. It's easier to coordinate events for men than to be responsible for really getting to know them. It's easier to advise a man biblically than to love a man biblically. It's easier to focus on what we know than actually being known ourselves. It's easier to talk about a process than to live out the process in community. It's easier to exercise authority and accountability than to extend affirmation and acceptance. It's easier to preserve our schedules than to reserve time for people in the midst of them. It's easier to point someone to a book for a solution than personally to be the solution *now*. It's easier to keep a safe distance than to be a safe harbor. It's easier to ask for men to "step up" for a mission than to step into their lives to minister. You get the point but just in case you don't, here it is: *there is no such thing as strong but relationally shallow men's ministry.*

> There is no such thing as strong but relationally shallow men's ministry.

Mind the gap.

Sticky Men

"I just don't understand," Bill said.

Accompanying these words were a red face and a frustrated expression. This men's ministry leader was hot under the collar with a burr under his shorts over the "lack of commitment" among the men of his church to help with a ministry project on an Indian reservation. He detailed the project for me, the compelling needs, and his heartbreak over the plight of their condition. After a few minutes I realized that his pain was self-inflicted. His anger was about his failure to keep his commitment to the people of the reservation—a commitment made without a strong personal network of relationships to support it. His message to the men of his church was, "This is something good all men should do, and doing it will be good for you." The men who were listening to him all but said by their nonresponse, "Get in line!" As in, get in line behind the plethora of other causes making the same requests from my small group, the kids ministry, the homeless shelter, the local school, via Facebook friends and from the hard recruiting team moms on all my kids' sports teams. He finally punctuated this seizure caused by the seeming lack of compassion in his fellowmen by saying, "And I sent them all a personal e-mail too." Let's review the facts.

1. No personal investment in any of the men
2. No conversations with them besides his project
3. No knowledge of their family makeup or commitments
4. No connections with them outside of church
5. No shared spiritual journeys or victories
6. No relational capital

No wonder.

Now meet Pete.

Pete tells me that he and all "his guys" are going downtown to partner with the church's motel ministry this weekend, and all of them are bringing their families! He has been meeting with them weekly as their "Get Healthy" group leader every Wednesday for the past twenty-four weeks. He has personally walked them through private struggles in their family, marital, and personal life. He has had them over to his house

> When you make authentic relational deposits, there is powerful relational capital to spend on strategic tasks.

on three different occasions for barbecues and football games. He finds time in his busy schedule as a real estate sales manager to meet with several of the guys one-on-one during the week. He has celebrated many victories of transformation and listened and counseled those same guys through repeated defeats.

These men are greeted every week by his now famous, "Hey bro, gimme some love" power handshakes, hugs, and affable Pacific Islander drawl. He opens God's Word with them. He prays with them. He does life with them. When Pete asked them to accompany him and his wife, Stacy, downtown, forty-eight of fifty-one of his guys went with him. What every pastor and man work-ing with men needs to learn from our man Pete is this: *when you make authentic relational deposits, there is powerful relational capital to spend on strategic tasks.*

Pete is *minding the gap* between success and failure very well.

When a church has a strong vision for the men, strong funnels that attract them, and a strong spiritual pathway but is failing to grow and reproduce, the first thing we examine is the relational dynamic between leaders and the men who have come *under their care.* With rare excep-tions, if that leader has paid the relational tax success requires in the form of investing personally in the lives of his men, knowing their jour-neys, and engaging them *outside of the formal structure,* then that leader produces what we call *sticky men.* That means that the relational bond has transcended the knowledge, sin management, and superficial levels of connection and morphed into something much more genuine—mas-culine intimacy. No other relationship in the Bible paints a picture of what this looks like more than the bond between David and Jonathan. It is the type of connection every man was made for and desires but few actually experience. It is forged not in the absence of pressure but *out of the real stresses and pressures* of life that men carry around but rarely share out of pride, fear, or shame. But somehow these two men were able to achieve that kind of authentic, strong, and courageous bond which neither blood nor death would ever be able to break. Both found the brother they never had and found him in God.

> Jonathan said to David, "Go in peace, for we have sworn friend-ship with each other in the name of the LORD saying, 'The LORD is witness between you and me and between your descen-dants and my descendants forever.'" (1 Sam. 20:42)

At the center was an awareness of the sovereignty of God which cre-ated their connection. Energizing the relationship was their mutual faith in God. Governing the relationship was the presence of God. And seal-ing their commitment was their accountability to God. That awareness, energy, faith, presence, and accountability on both sides produced a tran-scendent commitment that danger, depression, separation, isolation, and tribulation could not break. *That* is the type of connection the Sleeping Giant process seeks to produce among the men in your church. *That* is the revelation of what Scripture models and messages is possible in God for His men. *That* is the culture of commitment that will heal millions of men searching for divine connections, change the world, and power the church forward in a revolutionary way.

Imagine men in your congregation who do this with each other.

While David was at Horesh in the Desert of Ziph, he learned that Saul had come out to take his life. And Saul's son Jonathan went to David at Horesh and helped him find strength in God. "Don't be afraid," he said. "My father Saul will not lay a hand on you. You will be king over Israel, and I will be second to you. Even my father Saul knows this." The two of them made a covenant before the LORD. Then Jonathan went home, but David remained at Horesh." (1 Sam. 23:15–18)

Based on this snapshot we see that "sticky" men's culture is:

1. A culture of true concern
2. A culture of sacrifice
3. A culture of spiritual support
4. A culture of proactive encouragement
5. A culture that calls out men's gifting
6. A culture that speaks prophetically into men's lives
7. A culture that is sealed by spiritual bonds

8. A culture that refuels men for the spiritual and emotional battle

All the other pieces of the process may be in place, but if you do not pay close attention to the relational culture and quality of the relationships among the men, your results in the lives of men will suffer. If you don't do the relationships right, you will not do the process right. This principle is magnified a hundred times for the simple reason that men *prefer* to keep relationships on the surface but *crave authentic masculine connections.* Take a look at the benefits of Step 5 in the Sleeping Giant process.

A Strong Relational Core Allows For				
Modeling	Engaging	Listening	Praying	Calling Out
Initiating	Encouraging	Laughing	Advising	Commissioning
Caring	Educating	Leading	Admonishing	Confronting
Asking	Helping	Empathizing	Sharpening	Affirming
Entering	Giving	Talking Out	Stretching	Accepting
Directing	Promoting	Playing	Intervening	Rescuing

Later in the summary, use the dynamics mentioned in this table to rate the strength of the relational core in your men's ministry. We will ask you to rate it presently, and then we would like for you to rate it again on an annual basis to measure your progress. Just as all bodily motion and movement emanates from the core of your body, think of relational health among the men as the abdominal muscles of your men's ministry. While it might look strong from the outside, the strength of your relational core is always exposed when you have to rally the men toward a goal. The quicker they suit up and show up, the healthier your relational core. But if your men are slow to show or are no-shows, the muscles of your relational core have gotten flabby, and it is time for a checkup.

> The strength of your relational core is always exposed when you have to rally the men toward a goal.

The Sleeping Giant process *assumes* that men are hungry for masculine intimacy, approval, validation, and camaraderie. This assumption that men are looking for authentic and strong relationship tips the culture in favor of relationships over knowledge. After assessing the relational core of many churches, we have discovered that churches that emphasize a high knowledge measurement for their men usually have a weaker relational core. Not surprisingly, those churches that have an emphasis from top to bottom on strong

> Men learn best in a relational context of modeling, mentoring, and messaging.

relationship, transparency, and authentic connection among their ranks not only are more actionable but also have a high interest in leadership development and biblical knowledge. The simple fact is that when men perceive care, concern, interest, and excitement among their leaders, they receive instruction with greater efficiency and enthusiasm. The idea that a highly relational culture cannot be a highly disciplined and biblically literate culture is a myth based on our experience. Men learn best in a relational context of modeling, mentoring, and messaging. That goes for real fathers and sons as well as for spiritual fathers and sons.

Yet another excellent reason to aggressively *mind the gap.*

Leadership First

Millions of men are survivors.

I survived my own family's struggle with alcoholism. I survived being left alone to fight through the mine fields of my childhood, adolescent, and teenage years by myself. I survived economically, socially, relationally, and spiritually during those same years. I survived loneliness, rejection, and abuse. Miraculously, I survived the lure and bondage of addiction by the grace of God. I survived the slimy pits of fatherlessness and a broken quest for sonship. I survived the years of keeping all of these things to myself, never recognizing their toll on me, my relationships, and my ministry. I survived the sicknesses of character these secrets unleashed in my life. I survived the conduct flowing out of my sick character that would disconnect me from God and people. That's me. So why punish you with my past? Because my past patterns of thinking and living as a survivor dramatically impacted my ability to connect authentically with people as a man, as a husband, as a men's pastor, and as a leader. For men in general, and for me in particular, this relationship stuff is *hard.*

Survivors have to be loved back to health.

This is another good reason why we share our testimonies with other pastors: *most of them have never experienced the love of another man in a healthy way.* Not only is Step 5 in the Sleeping Giant process difficult to pull off with your leadership, it is difficult to pull off *as a pastor!* Thankfully, I have been refathered by God and by caring men in my life who love Christ who are pastors. As a result, I have been learning to extend the same care, concern, and fathering to other men around me including my leaders. But as a survivor, it has been a difficult but rewarding journey into health as a man. Both the stepping-stone and struggle of Step 5 in the Sleeping Giant process are highly personal and possibly life transforming. A leader of men cannot create relational health among his men from a place of relational unhealth within himself.

My message: *a strong relational dynamic starts with you.*

Once again, for ourselves and for the pastors we train, the lesson is: *you cannot give away what you do not possess.* The second lesson is: *your men's ministry leader cannot give away what he does not possess.* That is why all of our leaders have been through the GET IN and GET HEALTHY process themselves to deal with character issues and relational issues in a biblical way so they can be free and healed of what we call the "orphan spirit" that accompanies broken men into their relationships. Some call it "little man syndrome," and others call it a power trip, but it all feels and looks the same. Men with an orphan spirit need to feel a sense of control, be visible, and are afraid of up-close accountability. They also create deep fractures of unhealthiness among your men and in your church. "Rogue" men's ministries in churches are typically led by men with an orphan spirit. The only way to break that spirit is for the healing acceptance and love of God to flow directly into that man in the form of the Holy Spirit or through another man coming alongside to model and display God's love. Preferably, and most effectively, it comes from both sources. So many times churches stagnate with their men because they have an

> Men with an orphan spirit need to feel a sense of control, be visible, and are afraid of up-close accountability.

emotional orphan, survivor, or nonrelational man leading the ministry. *This is a deathblow for a men's ministry.* These men are great on providing the "truth" side of the ministry but are low on the "grace" side, the very thing men need to heal.

Grace and truth are out of balance—the two eternal powers that come from God to heal and save men from themselves, Satan, and sin. They are also the two character qualities that the God-man wants men to experience personally for themselves and then reproduce in the lives of other men. Take a look at the following diagram to see what we mean by having a strong relational core patterned after Jesus' character.

And the Word became flesh, and dwelt among us, and we saw His glory, glory as of the only begotten from the Father, full of **grace** and **truth**. (John 1:14 NASB, author emphasis)

Full of Grace and Truth among Men	
Grace	Truth
Acceptance	Authority
Affirmation	Accountability
Care	Confrontation
Concern	Challenge
Touch	Teach
Intimacy	Knowledge
Empathy	Responsibility
Love	Leadership
Support	Sharpening

These are the things every man needs to become healthy and to be able to give away health to others. These dynamics of grace and truth flowing one man to another are *powerful* and are *powerfully healing*. But in the end they must be modeled by you as the leader—a man who has

experienced the acceptance of God as well as
the authority of God on deep levels. It comes
to us on a spiritual level from God and is
realized on an emotional level when it comes
to us from another man in our lives. As the
leader not only do we need to mind the gap
between success and failure on the relational
health of our core men, but we must also
mind the gap in our own lives to ensure that
it gets modeled.

> **These dynamics of grace and truth flowing one man to another are powerful.**

Friendly voice. Specific reminder. Successful passage.
Mind the gap.

Key Learnings

- The more relational capital you have with your leadership, the more spiritual authority you have in their lives from God.
- The more relational capital your leaders have with the men coming into your process, the more spiritual authority they have with those men to bring them through the process and into leadership.
- The more relational capital you have flowing among your men, the faster they will respond to initiatives and needs in the church.
- The more relational health *you* have as a leader, the more Step 5 of the Sleeping Giant process will become a reality.

Chapter Fourteen

Step 6: Strong Alignment with Small Group Concepts

"Let us hold unswervingly to the hope we profess, for he who promised is faithful. And let us consider how we may spur one another on toward love and good deeds, not giving up meeting together, as some are in the habit of doing, but encouraging one another—and all the more as you see the Day approaching."

HEBREWS 10:23–25

The man sighed heavily and said, "God bless you!"

Grateful and relieved, the pastor who uttered those words was searching for a way to build a strong community of men in his church but was afraid he would have to either add to, alter, or amend his existing church structure in order to get one. He had his elders present, his men's ministry leaders, and his executive pastor watching him *convert to the Sleeping Giant model right in front of their eyes!* They were amazed that the number-one stakeholder in the church could be won over so completely. All the scenarios of resistance they had imagined, all the objections they thought he would raise, and all of their concerns over the amount of time it would take to move from intentions to actions *never materialized.* In one statement all of those fears evaporated and a grow-

> All initiatives need to be delivered to the congregation in a way that doesn't create or add a new structure on top of what already exists in the church.

ing optimism took their place. One dragon-slaying revelation and the battle everyone anticipated turned into a brotherhood of cooperation. One small area of pastoral risk strategically addressed up front and the plan for men goes supersonic in a stable way. So what did I say to create such a huge reversal of expectations? I said:

"You will not have to change anything about your church structure for this to happen."

The reason this is so significant is that all initiatives, in order to work, need to be delivered to the congregation in a way that *doesn't create or add a new structure on top of what already exists in a church.* Smart pastors consider this first when evaluating whether or not they want to incorporate any proposed initiative with their people. Smart pastors don't want to create another "ask," dilute church focus, or spend the precious relational capital they have accrued on something that does not drive the core vision forward. In the back of their minds, pastors are asking questions that individual ministries in a church do not have to consider. Questions like:

1. Will this new initiative or strategy be perceived as an additional commitment of time or an integrated part of an existing commitment of time?
2. Will the proposed initiative disrupt, in any way, our *existing* infrastructure by creating an *additional* infrastructure of people and programs?
3. Will the initiative have a positive impact on our existing initiatives and essential ministries, or will it compete with them for time, attention, visibility, people, and church resources?
4. Will the proposed strategy help us achieve our core vision and mission, or will it end up becoming a "club" for a small group of individuals with no greater purpose than serving their own needs?

5. Will the new ministry or "new angle" on an existing ministry cost me, the church, and church staff more in time, energy, and resources; or will it help free up or mobilize more of the same?

6. Is this "*good thing to do*" the enemy of the best way to advance our vision and mission?

Smart pastors demand answers to these questions before they commit to anything.

Once the pastor in my story sensed that the answer to these questions fit his considerations, a sense of relief and freedom to pursue the Sleeping Giant model in his church pervaded his spirit. In this case, he was reassured because the model is best delivered in churches that build their infrastructure around small group concepts and dynamics. By this we mean churches that *subgroup its members outside of the weekend services for the purposes of worship, fellowship, and discipleship.* What makes the small group different is that it seeks to take advantage of places *where men are already gathered or meeting.* While they go by various names and have subtle differences, the common denominator is drawing people from the congregation into smaller units to advance relational connections and foster accelerated spiritual growth.

Sunday School Groups	Grow Groups	Table Groups
Life groups	Small groups	Affinity groups
Community groups	Cell groups	Discipleship groups
Care groups	Home fellowships	Family groups

At Saddleback Church where I pastor the men, you cannot feel connected on a deep level at a weekend service. That's why I like telling the story about my pastor starting the church through a small group Bible study in his small condominium with seven people and then seeing how we are still committed to the small group concept as small groups just like that first one meet in thirty-five hundred homes all over southern California. I like the way Pastor Rick summarizes the power of small groups when he says: "It is impossible to feel connected to a crowd, even if that crowd is only fifty people. Crowds are great for worship, but they simply cannot provide the personal attention, encouragement, prayer support, listening ear, and accountability. I need those things. So do the people of your church. So do you."[21]

Key words: *So do you.*

Once again the integrity and simplicity of the Sleeping Giant model requires that the leaders practice personally what is implemented and taught tactically. That's what will make what follows meaningful versus hollow. Before we move on, it is important to ask you (the pastor, the leader of men, or the potential leader of men) a few simple questions that go to the integrity of process. Indulge us!

1. Who is paying close attention to your life as God's man?
2. Who is connecting with you as a husband (if you are married)?
3. Who is encouraging you personally?
4. Who is the listening ear when you need to vent or talk about something?
5. Who accepts and affirms you without judging you?
6. Who provides personal and spiritual accountability?
7. Who has permission to invade your space in Jesus' name?
8. Are *you* connected to other couples (if married) in small group community?

> The greatest relief a leader can experience— living out what the structure of the church is designed to produce spiritually.

Your enthusiasm for Step 6 in the Sleeping Giant process *publicly* will reflect the personal and practical value you place on Step 6 *privately.* We know it's personal, but the thrust of this step is getting a man into the highly personal and transformational setting of a small group. And *we want to make sure that man is you first!* That's the greatest relief a leader can experience—living out personally what the structure of the church is designed to produce spiritually.

So whether you have a Sunday school model, small group, or life group model, the goal is to have a safe place for men to start connecting and eventually start tracking into your leadership development pathway. Connecting with other men on a smaller scale not only achieves the goal of spiritual health but also provides the structure you need to care for him. Lastly, it provides a continuous and active connection point for new men reached by your ministry to start the process in your church. That's why at Saddleback Church we are always messaging to men in the congregation to "get in a group" based on their *relational context*. If they are married, we advise them to get in a group with other couples. If they are single, we advise them to meet in a small group with other singles. We tell them to get in a group because we know there will be a group of men *within that group* that they can start connecting with on a deeper level while being with others in their relational season of life. Our men's structure is purposed to work with and *not against* the church structure. But it wasn't always this way.

That's what we want to talk about next.

The Church Out of Alignment

"So if the men of our church are keeping secrets because their wives are present in the small group environment, is our church truly healthy even though we have large numbers of these groups?"

I dumped that nuclear bomb on my good friend and Saddleback couples pastor Todd Olthoff. I already knew the answer—an indisputable and resounding no. But *I had to ask this question*. Part of the reason why I *had* to ask it was due to the simple fact that we were launching hundreds of groups each September, husbands and wives were landing in small groups, and a dynamic had taken over in most of those groups. The men in those groups would not and could not discuss personal issues in front of the women in the group. This dynamic combined with the "iceberg" lifestyle of men revealing only the tips of their lives versus deal with the bigger issues underneath the surface is a reason for deep concern in any church.

Iceberg +
Gender Presence
= NO REVEAL

Really? Why a *deep concern?*

It's a deep concern because a Christian man keeping secrets in a body of believers is a roadside bomb that will eventually go off in a church. The inability to safely discuss pressures, temptations, and difficulties at home or on the job leads to a build-up of negative emotions.

> Satan can exploit and lie into a man's mind.

It's a deep concern because those unprocessed negative emotions distort reality and produce vulnerability in men for spiritual attack. It's a deep concern because Satan can exploit and lie into a man's mind living a double life *a lot better* than he can lie into a connected and confessing man walking in the light. It's a deep concern because secrets always sicken character, and a sick character will always be expressed in sick conduct and sin which destroys a man's connections to God and people. The following diagram shows this progression and reveals the basis for my question about the health of our men in small groups.

Secret Cycle

Secrets → Sicken Character → Sick Conduct and Sin → Broken Relationships with God & People

Men with Secrets in Churches → Sick Churches

When I posed this question to Todd, the men's ministry had a couple thousand guys in what we called "unique men's groups" that were separate and distinct from our couples groups. While this might appear like a healthy situation, it was not, and Pastor Todd was quick to drop his own bomb. He asked me: *"Is it healthy for one man to give advice to another man about his wife and marriage when he does not know the wife, never sees wife, and never interacts with the wife?"* Todd's point: transparency is only beneficial in the context of community, proximity of relationship, and knowledge of the people surrounding a man's life. In other words, men in these "unique men's groups" were providing advice *not* rooted in firsthand knowledge of the wife. By default, the

man being asked for advice only sees one side
of the story and slants the advice unfairly in
favor of the person he knows—the husband.
When the husband acts on advice presented to
him in this vacuum of relationship, it typically
backfires because his advisers were shooting
in the dark. Failing to hit the target, the wife
becomes suspicious that her husband's men's
group is something to be feared versus supported. She thinks: "Who
are these guys anyway?" To be fair, women do the same thing, and it is
just as unhealthy and unproductive. In the end, what you are left with
in many churches are couples battling the unseen phantoms called the
"Bible Study Friends" of their spouses. Just the way Satan likes it.

> **The problem?**
> *Competing
> communities.*

The problem? *Competing communities.*

Even though our church was a church of small groups—committed to getting people into relationship on a deeper and more meaningful level—we had an unhealthy dynamic flowing between our men's
community groups and couples community groups. Not only were
we competing for bodies in our groups, we were also competing for
calendar, for budget, for visibility, for priority, and for advocacy as
two distinct ministries within the same church. Unfairly caught in
the middle of all this energy and effort were the men of our church
who were forced to choose one or the other because of *limited time*.
Put between the rock and the hard place, men were choosing groups
that included their wives even though they would not experience the
transparency of the men's environment. Remember, *hundreds of these
groups were forming each fall.*

Let's summarize the dilemma:

1. Men in family or couples-based groups formed out of campaigns
   were keeping secrets.
2. Pure men's groups lacked the community needed with those connected to the men in those groups to provide healthy accountability and advice.
3. Men were forced to pick one or the other because of time limitations.

4. Ministries within the church experience the "silo" effect—indirectly competing versus cooperating for the health of the individual and diminishing the health of the church.

Make no mistake—good things are happening. People are coming to Christ, people are connecting and growing in small group community, and people are better off connected versus isolated. But Todd, Tom, myself, and our boss Steve Gladen (pastor of Small Group Community) were not satisfied with good. As pastors responsible for the sheep, we wanted maximum health for the man and for our church. We didn't want the "silo" effect. We didn't want ministries within the church competing against one another directly or indirectly. We didn't want our men isolated within their small groups, publicly meeting and privately suffering. We didn't want women being suspicious versus supportive of men's groups. And above all, we didn't want to fail in providing our pastor with qualified leaders born out of our own household to support the vision.

What happened next changed everything.

One Place for Men

Numbers don't lie.

The breakdown of men who were connected in groups was revealing. They were located by a three-to-one margin in couples or family-based groups over the pure men's groups. This was due in large part to the propensity of spiritual-growth campaigns to produce couples or family based groups almost exclusively. And while men's ministry had a healthy number of unique men's groups hovering around four hundred, the couples and family-based numbers swelled geometrically into the thousands with each spiritual growth campaign. But instead of feeling defeated by this trend, we kept searching for a way to use structure and the tendencies of men to solve some of these pervasive and unresolved problems mentioned earlier. Discouraged and almost out of ideas, I finally saw it. "Saw what?" you say. Listen *very closely*.

The Angle That Changed Everything

For every couples group or family group that forms, a women's and a men's group is also formed and are lying "dormant" within that group. We simply needed to train our existing couples and family-based groups to "subgroup" as men and women, resource them where they were, and provide bridges for those gender-based groups to connect to our leader-development pathway. *Men's groups were incubating inside of couples groups.* We needed to activate them, get the men connecting, and train future group leaders to subgroup intentionally by gender as a healthy behavior.

> For every couples group or family group that forms, a women's and a men's group is also formed.

This decision to *subgroup* men already in groups solved problems on almost every level.

1. It eliminated the need to have pure men's groups as a core strategy. If a man was married, we told him to join a couples group or a family group because we knew he would be encouraged to connect with the men of that group on a regular basis. If a man is married, "Get in a couples group" is the singular direction because we know he will be encouraged to subgroup and connect with the men in that group.

2. It eliminated the unhealthy dynamic of men keeping secrets. We would intentionally "subgroup" within these social networks so that men could address issues they were reluctant to mention in the presence of women.

3. Men were now in community with one another *and* in proximity to the spouses and children within the group. This provided for meaningful transparency and accountability because of the availability of the spouse to the friends.

4. The women would know the men in their husbands' men's group, know their wives, know their lives, and be more supportive of the connection versus suspicious.

5. Time—the most precious commodity a man has—is conserved by only having to commit to *one set of relationships and friendships* versus two sets. The man has a life group and men's group in one. The wife's needs are met, the man's needs are met, the couple's needs are met, and the children of the families are exposed to spiritual community.

6. The church escapes the "silo" effect, stops competing, and starts cooperating for the health of the individual and the health of the group.

7. Church health, group health, and individual health of members is accelerated dramatically.

Every church with small groups is sitting on a gold mine for men's ministry!

More important, a church built on small group community possesses the solid structure needed to direct people from the weekend structure which meets their need for worship, to the small groups structure which meets their need for fellowship, and into the leadership structure as men and women. Now you know why my pastor-friend at the beginning of the chapter was so relieved. He didn't have to change his structure at all to have an explosive and productive men's ministry. He just needed a *new angle* on his existing structure. The next generation of men's ministry in his church was already sitting there, incubating within his small groups structure waiting to be activated, directed, and mobilized.

He saw the Sleeping Giant and a new move of God for his church.

> Every church with small groups is sitting on a gold mine for men's ministry.

The following diagrams and descriptions show how a church can intentionally leverage its small group structure the way we did in order to grow an explosive, healthy, and leader-producing men's community. It also highlights the passages in the book of Acts that show the progression from house-to-house groups to men's subgrouping to the call of God upon men in those groups to pursue leadership in the church.

The Church in Alignment for the Men

Every day they continued to meet together in the temple courts. They broke bread in their homes and ate together with glad and sincere hearts, praising God and enjoying the favor of all the people. And the Lord added to their number daily those who were being saved. (Acts 2:46–47)

Location	Group Dynamic	People	Experience
Campus	Congregation	Everyone	Worship
Temple Courts			
Homes	Small Group	Men/Women	Fellowship
House to House	Introduce Men		Ministry
			Mission
Home/Other	Subgroup	Men	Fellowship
	Activate Men		Discipleship
			Ministry
			Mission
Start Relating	*Start Connecting*	*Start Supporting*	*Start Growing*

God Speaks in the Subgroup of Men

Among the prophets and teachers of the church at Antioch of Syria were Barnabas, Simeon (called "the black man"), Lucius (from Cyrene), Manaen (the childhood companion of King Herod Antipas), and Saul. One day as these men were worshiping the Lord and fasting, the Holy Spirit said, "Dedicate Barnabas and Saul for the special work to which I have called them." (Acts 13:1–2)

Men's Group Members	Experiences	Called by Holy Spirit to Lead
Barnabus	Worship	Barnabus
Simeon	Fellowship	Saul
Lucius	Discipleship	
Manaen	Ministry	
Saul	Holy Spirit	
	New Vision	

As men are encouraged to subgroup, start connecting, start pursuing relationship, and start cultivating a Christ-centered connection, the Holy Spirit will begin to raise up leaders out of those groups for leadership works on behalf of the church. At this point a church who has a well-communicated vision for men and spiritual pathway begins to collect the men God is calling and invites them into the next phase of life and leadership development. Men move from the subgroup meeting in homes or other locations to a centralized training program on campus *as an entire group or as individuals called out of that group into leadership community.* The following table shows this journey.

Called Men Intentionally Developed			
Location	Group Dynamic	People	Experience
Campus	Pathway Group	Men/Mentor	Fellowship
			Discipleship
			Ministry
			Mission
			Spiritual Pathway

Campus	Leader Community	Men/Pastors	Church Vision
			Encouragement
			Accountability
Campus	Ministry Leaders	Men/Men's Pastor	Men's Vision
Campus	Men's Leader Network	Men/Senior Pastor	Church Initiatives
Start Training	*Start Leading*	*Keep Training*	*Keep Leading*

Men have journeyed from the community to the crowd to the congregation to the committed to the core of church leadership. They came in through a men's funnel or the weekend funnel, got in a group, subgrouped with men in that location and started connecting and growing together. God's kingdom comes into that group of men, calls forth leaders from that group of men, and the church invites those men to experience the life and leader development pathway in a centralized and directed community of leaders on the church campus. The pathway is clear, strong, intentional, and rewarding. The pathway requires a commitment of time. The pathway is a combination of education and experiences. But by the end God's man is healthy, strong, and going with velocity into his mission. The effort taken to realign your efforts with men now begins to pay for itself in church health, church growth, and church mobility. The men's network is structurally connected from top to bottom as the following progression shows.

> The effort taken to realign your efforts with men now begins to pay for itself in church health, growth, and mobility.

The Men's Network

Senior Pastor

Men's Pastor

Men's Leaders

Men's Groups

Men of the Church

Men in the Community

Taking men along this journey is the story of the church from Jesus and the disciples to Paul and his disciples to you and your disciples. But like Paul we have to keep an eye on the men in our ranks, be consistent with the strategy, invest personally, and intervene prophetically to call out men as God is calling them already.

He came to Derbe and then to Lystra, where a disciple named Timothy lived, whose mother was a Jewess and a believer, but whose father was a Greek. The brothers at Lystra and Iconium spoke well of him. **Paul wanted to take him along on the journey,** so he circumcised him because of the Jews who lived in that area, for they all knew that his father was a Greek. As they traveled from town to town, they delivered the decisions reached by the apostles and elders in Jerusalem for the people to obey. **So the churches were strengthened in the faith and grew daily in numbers.** (Acts 16:1–5, author emphasis)

Maximum church health is achieved when the weekend structure is connected meaningfully to a small group structure which is aligned strategically for the sake of men. Not all churches are meeting house-to-house. But having studied and trained thousands of churches, we conclude the highest possibility for sustained and explosive growth of men in local churches happens in churches that are aligned with the small group concepts or house-to-house church movements. Once a man is in a group, it's now possible to move a man forward, message vision, and mentor a leader through the process. The integrity of this process requires great energy, great cooperation, and great sacrifice, but there is no disputing the product.

Great leaders.

Recommended Reading for This Chapter

Small Groups with Purpose: How to Create Healthy Communities by Steve Gladen (www.stevegladen.com)

This practical book, written by my friend and fellow Saddleback Pastor Steve Gladen, walks you through the questions you need to answer to develop your own intentional small group strategy. It is a step-by-step process that can be implemented in any size church. Steve's tribal knowledge will save you years of time and allow you to implement the Sleeping Giant model in the most effective way.

To see small group tools and resources scan this QR code with your mobile device or go to lifeway.com/kennyluck.

Key Learnings

- Your men's ministry must drive the core vision and structure of your church forward.
- Men's ministry is best delivered in the context of small group dynamics or a modified model that advances masculine connection where encouragement, prayer, and accountability can happen.
- Leaders must be the first to adopt and demonstrate behaviorally the spiritual mission you wish to teach tactically.
- The inability of men to discuss pressure, temptations, and challenges at home may lead to pent-up emotions that manifest negatively with others.
- The creation of silos in your ministries may lead to competition for resources, budget, and visibility that could negatively affect your church's mission.

- The single largest source of connected men already exists in your couples ministry where men are already in relationship with one another waiting to be mobilized.
- The intentional developmental pathway encompasses a mixture of exposing men to education, providing experiences for them, and giving them a place to express their gifts and abilities.

Chapter 15

Step 7: Strong Consistency of Culture

I will tell you what I want and what I have on my heart. Take men that have gifts and train them for this work of reaching the people. I believe we have got to have gap men, men who stand in the gap between the ministers and the laity.

D. L. Moody

"Bill, meet your new best friend."

Scott was intentionally putting himself, his time, and his life on the line to *enter another man's life and make sure he would be helped.* Those words were followed by a handshake, an exchange of information, and an uneasy but exciting anticipation at what the relationship from this moment forward would hold. You see, just moments before Bill had walked out of the weekend service and come over to the men's ministry kiosk in a daze. Stunned by his wife's announcement the night before that if things didn't change she would be gone, Bill was suffering from shell shock. He couldn't hear anything. He couldn't see any solutions. He couldn't surmise what went wrong. He was completely disoriented emotionally. He had no guy friends that could offer him depth of understanding. His professional networks, business associates, and golfing buddies weren't exactly cut out to help with stuff like this. Desperate and searching, Bill landed at church as an emotional placeholder; he couldn't remember a word of the message but felt that urge to turn to God however feebly he could. He drove by Saddleback Church every day on his commute back and forth to work. On the weekends he saw the cars going in and out like an ant colony, and most days he would mentally write off all the activity he saw as good "for people who need that kind of support." But this was not one of those days, and showing up in a house of worship was the last thing he thought he would ever be doing.

And yet here he was.

He was asking what any man in his shoes would ask himself.

- What now?
- Whom do I call?
- How do I fix this?
- Whom do I tell?
- Who will find out?
- What's the process?
- Is there anybody who can help me?
- Should I just leave?

For a man who was so smart, so outwardly successful, so resourceful, and so put together materially, he sure felt stupid and out of place at church—the very place he viewed as a crutch for weak people. But stripped of his pride and facing separation, his attitude had dramatically changed in the last twenty-four hours. Self-absorbed and drunk on his own confusion, he wandered out of the worship service, and a sign caught his eye: *"Men's Ministry . . . Stronger Together."* Bill's pain had given him a new set of glasses to see what he never thought about or wanted to seek just the day before—help. Inexorably and unexplainably he found himself standing in front of the kiosk and under the sign staring at a well-dressed guy in a Tommy Bahama shirt who reminded him of his business partner.

"Men's Ministry . . . Stronger Together"

Scott meets Bill.

What Bill did not know at that moment but would find out shortly was that Scott had been in his shoes just three years prior. Scott had been standing in the same place where Bill was in every way, on every emotional level, and at the same level of loss and confusion. In his desperation Scott dragged himself onto our campus and chanced a conversation on the patio where the guy on the other side of the table told him about the *"Men's Core Health"* classes meeting on campus which included one entitled *"Being God's Man by Understanding a Woman's Heart."* Out of options and with his own marital ultimatum looming over his life, Scott wrestled with and temporarily pinned his own ego down long enough to show up for that small group. Not knowing what to expect and afraid he would be asked to sing, socialize awkwardly, or share, his defenses were up. Other men poured in, and four strangers filled up his table in the classroom. The facilitator then told the guys to introduce themselves, tell the other guys how long they had been going to Saddleback, and (get this) describe the year, make, and model of their first car along with one special feature that stood out about the car. Scott loved his 1979 Triumph TR6 and comfortably began connecting with other men that would walk with him for the next eight months. Scott's "problem" from his past was now going to be used by God in the present to comfort and help Bill.

> Burn these two words on your brain: *meaning* and *context*.

"Bill, meet your new best friend."

Resonating and Reproducing

Burn these two words on your brain: *meaning* and *context*.

So often we fret over the content, curriculums, or methodologies of how we are doing things and forget that stuff doesn't matter to a man who's drowning in private pain or realizing that self-preservation isn't a purpose. What matters is what your ministry to men *means to him in his context.* The beauty of an organically reproducing and resonating men's culture is that the men who have experienced it personally (in their context as a man) will confidently recommend it interactively with other men in a similar context. That is what happened between Bill and Scott. Scott remembers the short-lived but real awkwardness of personal entry. He remembers discovering meaningful people and a clear process. He recalls being challenged to move beyond resolution of his problem to reproduce his transformation in others. He knows where he has been and how far he has come. He sees himself in Bill as a man and as a husband. More important, he knows the process works.

Meaning and *context*.

> Your men's ministry must have the breadth and width to meet any man that encounters it meaningfully and in his context as a man.

The principle is this: your men's ministry must have the breadth and width to meet any man that encounters it meaningfully and in his context as a man. Whether it is in the context of a problem or a struggle to find his purpose in life. Men in your church who have confidence in and personal knowledge of the process is the invisible intangible of a fully orbed, resonating, and reproducing men's ministry. Scott's words to Bill about meeting his "new best friend" speak volumes about the ministry standing behind him, which *stands ready to do for Bill what it did for him*. Who says that to another man in the first twenty minutes of a conversation? A *confident* man, that's who! A man who has *experienced* healing for himself. Scott's eagerness to extend himself personally reflects the clarity and quality of a solid vision, a strong spiritual pathway, and a powerful relational core that delivers for men in need. It also reflects a ton of sacrifice and skin in the game on the part of the leaders who are constantly monitoring and managing the core pieces and steps to ensure the vision and delivery systems are intact.

Bill will follow in Scott's footsteps because the Sleeping Giant process, once it is built and implemented with integrity over time, becomes it's own self-reproducing entity apart from the leadership. And that is the goal, isn't it? That means every man who comes through having your vision for the ministry deeply and relationally implanted in his mind and life. Men who feel intuitively that the goal is to see every man in the congregation and in the community connected to a healthy men's small group. Men who have a story to tell, are living Christ-centered lives, and are motivating others to do the same. Men who are fulfilling the Great Commandment and Great Commission publicly, proudly, and naturally because that's what the process is purposed to produce. Specifically, it produces men like Scott who are standing in the gap between the pastors of the church and the people in the congregation and community *doing the ministry of the church* every day. Doing it not under compulsion but in their context as men, as husbands, as professionals, as fathers, as neighbors, and as strugglers who have had an experience worth sharing with others. Every man is a minister within the priesthood of believers.

THAT is what you are shooting for.

So let's track Scott's thinking through the process as a men's ministry leader doing the ministry. As we do this, remember that Scott is not think-ing methodology or pathways or processes. He is creating meaning and con-text for the man in front of him. We want to see how it rolls out practically not intellectually. We want you *to see* the answer to the following questions.

- What masculine meaning and context are being tapped?
- What is the man actually experiencing in the process?
- What essential ministry principles are being emphasized?
- What biblical truths or principles are being witnessed?
- What tools are being used?
- How long does he remain in each step of the process?
- What results are we looking for?

Scott experienced each of the following phases. More personally, he is counting on the same dynamics to serve Bill the same way it served him. Scott's conversation with Bill about his marriage and offer to help begins phase one. Here's what's going on organically through the men's culture at Saddleback and will become realities in your church as you apply Sleeping Giant principles.

Phase 1: Proactively Defining and Meeting Needs

Felt Needs of Men	Principles	Biblical Values
Purpose	Touch need/pain	"Hungry?" Feed.
Marital Health	Transform his life	"Naked?" Clothe.
Sexual Integrity	Take down the pathway	Matthew 25:35
Family Health		
Authentic Friendships		
Significance		
Character Growth		

Outcomes Sought	Tools Used Here
Connects to other men	Get Healthy Curriculum/DVDs
Connects to men's ministry	"Intimacy"
Feels helped	"Temptation"
The spiritual pathway is explained	"Family"
Goes to the next core health class	"Friendship"
Character issues addressed	

Vision Cast

1 Timothy 3 Leader Requirements Met

Being tracked relationally through the pathway

Key Result

The helped and transformed man wants to know: "What's next?"

Duration

32 Weeks

Phase 2: Discipling for Depth

Leader Needs	Principles	Biblical Values
Spiritual Formation	Integrity of heart	Luke 6:40
Spiritual Disciplines	Integration of life	Colossians 1:28–29
Leadership Training	Involvement in experiences	Colossians 2:6–8
Biblical Worldview		
Leadership Experiences		
Gifting Identified		
Call to Ministry		

Outcomes Sought	Tools Used Here
Leader is selected	Get Strong Curriculum/DVDs
Leader is called	Risk (faith)
Leader is being trained	Dream (Christlikeness)
Leader is being mentored	Fight (spiritual warfare)
Leading a small group	Soar (Holy Spirit)
Joining leadership community	Foundations

Key Result

The helped and transformed man wants to know: "What's next?"

Duration

32 Weeks

Phase 3: Deploy to Lead

Assignment Needs	Principles	Biblical Values
Church small group leader	Responsible for men	2 Timothy 2:2
Get Healthy class facilitator	Reproducing leaders	Matthew 28:18–20
Men's Ministry Leader	Replacing Staff	Romans 15:20
Church Ministry Leader		Ephesians 2:10
High School Leader		
Kids Ministry Leader		
Missions Team Leader		
Men's Pastor in Another Church		

Outcomes Sought	Tools Used Here
In a men's group	Leadership Books
Leading a men's group	Devotional Books
Part of Leadership Community	Training Seminars
Recruiting New Leaders	Spiritual growth tools
Teaching Pathway	Leadership Assessment tools
Training Others	
Cross Trained	
Spiritual Health Plan	
Continuing Education	

Key Result

The reproducing leader asks, "Who else can I bring along the journey?"

Duration

Lifetime

These three phases are the *functional dynamics* of GET IN, GET HEALTHY, GET STRONG, and GET GOING that provide the real meaning and context for the philosophical architecture. This is what the ministry should look like, feel like, sound like, live like, project and reflect *practically*. This is the intuitive process and the theological applications of quality men's ministry in our view. These are the results we are watching for and demanding out of our leaders at each phase. These are the tools we have landed on and perfect using. This is what we model by example and message between the lines. It is not passed out in a document, and the only place you will see these put on paper is right here in this book. Most important, this is the culture of consistency that breeds confidence in our deployed men like Scott that fuels their confidence as they talk to the Bills of the congregation and in the community.

Thus, *"Bill, I am your new best friend."*

Everyman to Equipped Leader

Bill is everyman.

He presents himself to us, and it is our job to engage him proactively, ask good questions, listen to his responses, and discern what he needs help with *now* in order to provide the meaning and context critical to begin the journey. He might come to us through a response card put in the offering basket during the weekend service. He may wander toward our table on the patio after a weekend service. He might be the husband of a frantic wife who calls us after hours. He could be the friend of a friend who wants to plug him into a local church. He could be a disoriented husband in search of counseling. He could be the uncooperative husband who has been issued an ultimatum. He could be the business executive who possesses everything he ever wanted but has no one to share it with. He could be the unfulfilled hedonist who is tired of waking up dehydrated and with a headache. But regardless of who he is, where he is coming from, and how he lands, your men who encounter him can't be timid, confused, or hesitant when it comes to meeting his needs. They have to *know*.

Know what?

They have to know that your culture and process are solid. They have to know that if they refer him into the process he will be taken care of. They have to know that the relational strength that stood out to them when they came into the ministry is still alive and well. They need

> They have to know that your culture and process are solid.

to know that he is going to be transformed. They need to know that he will be challenged to take hold of a vision that is larger than just the solving of his problem. They need to know that God is waiting for him amid the community of men and will call him to lead. They need to know that he will soon join the ranks of God's men in leader community. They need to know that the ministry behind him will meet the needs of the man in front of him. They need to know those things because it informs their attitude and their actions in that *first touch*.

With this knowledge your men can start asking questions courageously and confidently.

- Do you live nearby?
- How did you find out about our church?
- Married?
- Got kids?
- How can I help you today?
- What do you need right now?
- Are you currently in a group?
- Are you a member?
- Do you have a group a group of guys around you helping figure things out?

The goal is to identify his greatest need, meet him there, and help him take the next right step versus force-fit him into your church context in ways he's not looking for. Then, based on the information he has given, you can offer this man the right next step. This will look like one or more of the following:

- Couples small group
- Singles small group
- Get Healthy class
- Lay counseling

- Celebrate Recovery
- Large group Bible study

The goal in recommending and walking him to one of these locations is to meet his need and connect him to the pathway. This action always starts with getting him into a small group setting. Once there, he experiences the church defining and meeting his deepest felt needs as a man, calling him into a discipleship relationship and process, and commissioning him to serve the body and share Christ. This is implicit, intuitive, and integral.

Amazingly, Bill goes from everyman to an equipped leader on mission.

Just remember that this picture took us years to develop. And while we hope our pain is your gain, here are a few critical factors to keep in mind as you implement the Sleeping Giant model in your church and begin working with the Bills in your congregation and community.

- Timing is a four- to five-year window to fully implement the Sleeping Giant model.
- The model requires a dedicated leader within your church who has a kingdom assignment and gifting with men that includes spiritual gifts, passion, character, skills, and testimony of men's ministry in his own life.
- There is no "pole vaulting" from Step 1 to Step 6. Each step incrementally builds on and supports the subsequent step.
- Leaders are advised to launch the process among themselves first or join the first wave group beginning the process.
- Pastoral support and sign-off are essential
- The model must fit within, alongside, and cooperate with your church structure.
- Your men's leaders are constantly asking:
    - Who are we developing and bringing along?
    - How can I develop them?
    - What experiences can I involve them in?
- It is successful if you can walk away, and it continues to be productive and reproduce leaders.

> The Sleeping Giant model is only as good as your understanding of the commitment required.

The Sleeping Giant model is only as good as your understanding of the commitment required. However, any church that is realistic, diligent, and invested in men can deliver it well because it is principle driven and relationally fueled. The only thing left now is to get a clear picture of the current condition of your men's ministry, assess what is missing or needs improvement, and then chart a simple course for the future. We are going to help you with that by letting you find yourself in the following profiles contained in chapter 16. Then we want you to take the online assessment and put together a simple and meaningful plan of action you can pursue based on your church's needs and structure.

It is now time to wake the Sleeping Giant.

Key Learnings

- You must find the men in your church who are willing to sacrifice their time in order to enter other men's lives in a meaningful way.
- We are searching to identify and engage what God has already placed in men's hearts.
- A man's pain is a doorway to be able to minister to him and often is the impetus for him seek something.
- A man who has walked the similar path is ideal to reaching other hurting men, as he can help bring meaning and context and knows the process.
- Your men's ministry must have a structure that meets needs and bridges men into leadership out of meeting that need into a meaningful ministry.

- PHASING
  - Phase 1: Proactively define and meet needs.
  - Phase 2: Disciple for depth.
  - Phase 3: Deploy to lead.
  - As dynamics of *GET IN, GET HEALTHY, GET STRONG, GET GOING.*
- Ultimately, *solving the problem* is not as primary as connecting men to God. Taking a man to his next incremental steps will get him there.
- You know the process is successful when men are reaching other men organically and it continues to reproduce leaders.

Chapter 16

Where Are You in the Process?

If the ax is dull and its edge unsharpened, more strength is needed, but skill will bring success.

ECCLESIASTES 10:10

"What do we do first?"

If you have read this far, you are probably ready to take some simple steps forward. So let's get to it and begin the process of asking some questions, providing honest answers, scoring your responses, and seeing some concrete steps that will advance your efforts with the men of your church. Here's the process.

1. **Reflect honestly.** Tom has designed some questions for you to work through that will provide us with a starting point for your church on a no-nonsense basis for your action plan.
2. **Recognize reality.** There is no good or bad or right or wrong in the Sleeping Giant assessment process. There is only truth and reality. That's the best place to begin the process. Churches, for example, that have little to nothing happening will stop scoring points after the first few questions. Others will score on most questions. It is only essential that the score reflect reality. You cannot change what you don't acknowledge.

209

3. **Respond practically.** Based on your score, we will be able to provide scenarios that match where you are and suggest specific pathways of action for you to consider.

The revelation has been provided. The response begins *now*.

Sleeping Giant Locator Assessment

A) Our church clearly understands the unresolved issues our men are facing. (circle one)
   a. Untrue   0
   b. Mostly untrue   1
   c. Neutral   2
   d. Mostly True   3
   e. True   4

B) Our church prioritizes the impact and acts on the key issues facing our men. (circle one)
   a. Untrue   0
   b. Mostly untrue   1
   c. Neutral   2
   d. Mostly True   3
   e. True   4

C) Our church provides experiences that involve the men and link them to an intentional developmental process. (circle one)
   a. Untrue   0
   b. Mostly untrue   1
   c. Neutral   2
   d. Mostly True   3
   e. True   4

D) Our church communicates in ways that resonate with men and cause them to activate or connect with the church. (i.e., Men become men in the company of other men.) (circle one)
   a. Untrue   0
   b. Mostly untrue   1

  c. Neutral   2
  d. Mostly True   3
  e. True   4

E) Our church has a regularly scheduled men's breakfast or meeting. (circle one)
  a. None   0
  b. Weekly   4
  c. Quarterly   3
  d. Bi-Yearly   2
  e. Yearly   1

F) Our men's breakfast or meeting intentionally connects men to small groups. (circle one)
  a. Untrue   0
  b. Mostly untrue   1
  c. Neutral   2
  d. Mostly True   3
  e. True   4

G) Our men's breakfast or meeting has teaching where men's lives are changing for the better. (circle one)
  a. Untrue   0
  b. Mostly untrue   1
  c. Neutral   2
  d. Mostly True   3
  e. True   4

H) There is evidence that men have connected as a result of our men's breakfast/meeting. (circle one)
  a. Untrue   0
  b. Mostly untrue   1
  c. Neutral   2
  d. Mostly True   3
  e. True   4

I) Men are engaging in weekly Bible studies and other men's offerings. (circle one)
    a. Untrue   0
    b. Mostly untrue   1
    c. Neutral   2
    d. Mostly True   3
    e. True   4

J) Our church provides topical classes that address the needs of men. (circle one)
    a. Untrue   0
    b. Mostly untrue   1
    c. Neutral   2
    d. Mostly true   3
    e. True   4

K) Our events, classes, and Bible studies for men connect men to small groups. (circle one)
    a. Untrue   0
    b. Mostly untrue   1
    c. Neutral   2
    d. Mostly true   3
    e. True   4

L) Our church has regularly scheduled events for men. (circle all that apply) DEMOGRAPHICS ONLY—UNSCORED
    a. Participation Sports (basketball, golf, softball, etc.)
    b. Father/Child Events
    c. Annual Retreat or Conference
    d. Quarterly Meeting/Rally
    e. Topical Seminars (i.e., finances, spiritual leadership in the home)
    f. Attending Sporting Event Together
    g. Weekly Bible Study
    h. Other Events Not Listed Above

M) Our church has: (circle all that apply) DEMOGRAPHICS
ONLY—UNSCORED
    a.   Weekend Services
    b.   Midweek
    c.   Sunday School
    d.   Small Groups
    e.   Men's Small Groups

N) We have established direction, purpose, and goals (mission and/or
vision) for our men's ministry. (circle one)
    a.   Untrue   0
    b.   Mostly untrue   1
    c.   Neutral   2
    d.   Mostly True   3
    e.   True   4

O) The men's direction, purpose, and goals (mission and/or vision) are
consistent with our church's mission and vision. (circle one)
    a.   Untrue   0
    b.   Mostly untrue   1
    c.   Neutral   2
    d.   Mostly True   3
    e.   True   4

P) The direction, purpose and goals (mission and/or vision) of the
men's ministry and can be stated by the men of the ministry. (circle
one)
    a.   Untrue   0
    b.   Mostly untrue   1
    c.   Neutral   2
    d.   Mostly True   3
    e.   True   4

Q) We have a documented and communicated developmental pathway
that our men can and have shared with others. (circle one)
    a.   Untrue   0
    b.   Mostly untrue   1

    c.   Neutral   2

    d.   Mostly True   3

    e.   True   4

R) Our church has an effective leader development process for men where the results are men actively serving in the church. (circle one)

    a.   Untrue   0

    b.   Mostly untrue   1

    c.   Neutral   2

    d.   Mostly true   3

    e.   True   4

S) Our men's leaders are constantly reproducing and raising new leaders. (circle one)

    a.   Untrue   0

    b.   Mostly untrue   1

    c.   Neutral   2

    d.   Mostly true   3

    e.   True   4

T) The majority of our groups are facilitated/taught by: (circle one)

    a.   Pastors   1

    b.   Elders   2

    c.   Volunteers   3

    d.   All the above   4

U) Our developmental pathway for men is known and can be/has been communicated to others by our men. (circle one)

    a.   Untrue   0

    b.   Mostly untrue   1

    c.   Neutral   2

    d.   Mostly true   3

    e.   True   4

V) Our developmental pathway is well known to the men and is aligned with the values and processes of our church. (circle one)

    a.   Untrue   0

    b.   Mostly untrue   1

    c. Neutral   2
    d. Mostly true   3
    e. True   4

Quantify Outcomes

Place an "X" by each segment as to whether you have it or not. It will help you see quantitatively what you have and don't have.

Segments	No	Yes
Pancake Breakfast		
Events		
Topical Classes		
Programs (Bible Studies)		
Groups		
Pathway		
Leader Pathway		
Reproducing Leaders/Pipeline		
Servant Teachers/Facilitators		
Vision		

Scoring Scenarios and Suggested Action Steps

SCENARIO 1

Score: 0–16

Description: No or infrequent meetings and/or connection places. No strategy or plans for men.

Action Plan:

- Meet with Pastor to understand the mission and vision.
- Conduct Magic Wand meeting with pastor and men's ministry leaders or potential leaders to determine desired outcomes.
- Identify "funnel" events as a place to gather men.

SCENARIO 2

Score: 17–28

Description: Breakfasts, events, and classes, no vision implemented, no leader development, and no pathway.

Action Plan:

- Implant vision and mission (start using the language of your vision) to the men as part of your event.
- Use the "funnel" event to connect men to one another (sit at tables).
- Use discussion questions and talk time to get the guys used to interacting with one another about significant matters.

SCENARIO 3

Score: 29–37

Description: Programs (Bible studies), events, classes, no groups, no leader development, no pathway, and no vision implemented.

Action Plan:

- Gather rosters from funnel events and challenge to meet again outside of event.
- Seed known group leaders or those you believe could lead a group of guys to connect from funnel events.
- Create an intentional developmental pathway with your existing leadership.
- Develop a formal "funnel" strategy to move men from attendance to connection.
- Develop a leader selection process from the men that are currently moving through the process. These are your future leaders.

SCENARIO 4

Score: 38–66

Description: Program (Bible studies), events, classes, groups, no pathway, no vision implemented, and leader development.

Action Plan:

- Share intentional development pathway for the men that attend.
- Share the vision and mission each and every time they meet.
- Challenge men to take initial steps now in their spiritual growth and plant the seed that will lead to leader development as they move from GET HEALTHY to GET STRONG.
- Host a Sleeping Giant training event.

- Begin forming a relational support structure to support forming groups from pastor to coaches/mentors to group leaders.
- Start to develop facilitators for additional men's small groups on campus studies. Share facilitation.
- Challenge every leader to bring along men that are taking their next leadership step. Mentor those identified as potentials.

SCENARIO 5

Score: 67 +

Description: Program (Bible studies), events, classes, groups, pathway aligned with values and process for leader development, reproducing leaders, and vision—full integration.

Action Plan:

- The challenge for you will be consistency of culture, encouragement of leadership, and creative ways to get more men into the funnel. Continue to run connection events to keep filling and launching new groups.
- I would strongly recommend Kenny coming to your church and conducting a conference. He will support your process and activate the new men you invite to get connected to your pathway. He has personally connected tens of thousands of men into a life and leader development process.
- I would also encourage you to look at the GET HEALTHY and GET STRONG tools connected to the Sleeping Giant pathway. We are always looking for great tools and ways to stay current and fresh in our process with men.

Staying Connected

Tell us what you think. What has worked for you? Share stories with us. Ask questions. Join the network of churches that are using Sleeping Giant. We want to hear from you!

For Speaking or Conferences
Kenny Luck
kennyl@everymanministries.com
kennylu@saddleback.com
www.everymanministries.com

For Sleeping Giant Training
Tom Crick
tomc@saddleback.com

Notes

[1] "Where Have All the Good Men Gone?" *The Wall Street Journal*, February 19, 2011.

[2] "Man Up! Rethinking Masculinity," *Newsweek*, September 27, 2010.

[3] "The End of Men," *The Atlantic*, July/August 2010.

[4] Alessandra Staley, "Downsized and Downtrodden, Men Are the New Women," *The New York Times*, October 10, 2011.

[5] Anya Kamenetz, "The Case for Girls," *Fast Company*, December 2011/January 2012, 122–30.

[6] Dr. Philip Zombardo, "The Demise of Guys," presented at the TED Conference, March 2011; video at www.ted.com/talks/lang/en/zimchallenge.html.

[7] Richard Corliss, "Land of the Lost: Delusions of Manhood," *TIME*, June 15, 2009.

[8] William Bennett, "Why Men Are in Trouble," CNN.com, October 4, 2011.

[9] 2010 Report on the Global AIDS Epidemic.

[10] Ibid.

[11] International Justice Mission Factsheet, www.ijm.org/resources.

[12] Ibid.

[13] Andrew Cockburn, "21st Century Slaves," *National Geographic*, September 2003.

[14] "UNICEF Progress for Children: A Report Card on Child Protection," no. 8, September 2009.

[15] Ibid.

[16] U.S. State Department, Report on Trafficked Persons, 2009.

[17] "Not Another Minute More: Ending Violence Against Women," 2003 UNIFEM report.

[18] 2009 U.S. Census Bureau Report.

[19] See   edsitement.neh.gov/lesson-plan/hans-christian-andersens-fairy-tales.

[20] Robert Coleman, *The Master Plan of Evangelism* (Grand Rapids: Revell, 2006).

[21] Steve Gladen, *Small Groups with Purpose* (Grand Rapids: Baker, 2011), 8.

HCSB

Take a fresh look

Every word matters.

Every word of Scripture matters because every word is from God and for people. Because every word is from God, the HCSB uses words like Yahweh (Is. 42:8), Messiah (Luke 3:15), and slave (Rev. 1:1). And because every word of Scripture is for 21st century people, the HCSB replaces words like "Behold" with modern terms like "Look." For these reasons and others, Christians across the globe are taking a fresh look at the HCSB.

HCSB
Every Word Matters
HCSB.org

Need help waking the sleeping giant in your church?

If you're looking to start a men's ministry in your church, or to put some life back into an existing one, the *Sleeping Giant* study is the first and most important tool you'll need. It all begins with the pastor and his vision for the church. He recruits a core team of men and shares that vision (or develops one with the help of the team). They then spend six weeks together learning, modeling, and practicing the principles of this new strategy through the *Sleeping Giant* core-team experience. This includes video, discussion questions, group activities, case studies, and dynamic group interaction. The result is a leadership engine dedicated to fulfilling the pastor's vision.